# The New Entrepreneurz

# The New Entrepreneurz

## Changing the Way You Play Life

Ronen Gafni and Simcha Gluck

WILEY

# CONTENTS

*Introduction*                                                    *vii*

**1**   **Ronen Tells the Story behind FreshBiz**           1

**2**   **The New Entrepreneurz**                            17

**3**   **What Game Are You Playing?**                       47

**4**   **Win to the Winth Power**                           71

**5**   **Action Cards**                                     79

**6**   **Green Titles and Red Titles**                      97

**7** Smart Business                                        113

**8** All-in                                               141

**9** Teaser: You've Already Won the Game                  159

**10** Solving the World's Greatest Problem                177

   *Interviews*                                            *183*

   *Acknowledgments*                                       *231*

   *Index*                                                 *235*

# INTRODUCTION

**Figure I.1**  Todd Goodman

## Who Are the New Entrepreneurz?

They are the game changers who can be found playing different games across the spectrum. They are the business owners, the managers, the lawyers, the moms and dads, the lovers, the educators, the artists, and the healers.

Entrepreneurship is no longer just about business; it is the new mind-set.

Imagine this: You live on an island where you know everyone, you're familiar with the little shops and the schools, and you know exactly how everything works. Lately, things have started to become polluted; occasionally there's a natural disaster, but overall, it's familiar and comfortable and the place you call home.

Despite this, you feel a sense of something looming in the background, of something being not quite right anymore, perhaps something breaking. You choose to climb a hard-to-reach mountain: You'd like to meditate and breathe some fresh air. But upon reaching the peak, you notice for the first time, across the sparkling waters, another green, lush island.

Wow! Until that moment you were aware only of yourself and the little island where you'd grown up and to which you'd been confined. You had no idea there was another whole world out there, a New Island of potential and possibility that you could aspire to reach. Taking out your super-high-definition smartnoculars, you notice something very interesting about the New Island.

Although it appears that the New Islanders share the same technology and resources as your island, what is very different over there is the *way* the New Island citizens are using the technology and resources. They seem to operate according to a different set of rules, beliefs, and guidelines. You're awed as you watch them generate extraordinary results, create far better solutions, and express themselves creatively in ways you hadn't thought possible . . . until now.

It dawns on you that the reason people on your island can't achieve the same outcomes despite having the same potential is because they're blocked by their own outdated mind-sets. After weeks of observing the New Island, you see that it also faces challenges and troubled waters from time to time. But the people there always meet these challenges with ease, collaborations, and what seems like a mind-set of genuine serious playfulness.

By now, you are really excited about the idea of joining that New Island, but how are you going get the new set of skills that will help you make that shift in mind-set? The good news is that we're here to help you with that.

So let's cross over to the New Island . . . the New Entrepreneurz style!

In this book you won't find secret formulas, magic incantations, or a one-size-fits-all approach. We don't believe in such things on the road to self-expression and true entrepreneurship. What works for one person won't necessarily work for another, and where one person is heading isn't necessarily where you want to be headed. So your job is to mark the X on your map, and your quest is to find your own unique way there. This book is simply here to teach you how to read the map, equipping you with the smartnoculars that let you spot both opportunities and threats, and with a sword to fight your inner and outer dragons. Now you can build the bridge and cross over to the New Island . . . as a New Entrepreneur.

So build the bridge, cross it, and really experience what life on that New Island feels like by bringing the talents that *you* have, fully into the picture.

## Don't Read This Book; Live It!

That's because this book is not about *in*formation. It's about *trans*formation.

Over the past few decades, the world went from being about stuff and having stuff to being about information and having information. The Information Age has been awesome because it unlocked for us unlimited access to everything we could want to have and know. Now we are rapidly heading into the Transformation Age, where having and knowing is nowhere near as significant as *being*. Being and experiencing life to the fullest is what the New Entrepreneurz are all about, and they look to do so with the right tools, skills, and mind-set.

*Entrepreneurial thinking* is the ability to turn ideas into reality, and over the course of this book when we refer to entrepreneurs, we really mean *entrepreneurial thinkers*. We never reference people who only build businesses because no one in the world *only* builds businesses. People have never been more multidimensional, wearing various hats, taking on numerous projects, and simultaneously existing in and operating multiple games across the spectrum.

Here is some fun information regarding the authors. Ronen has many dimensions; he's a great cook, a programmer, an awesome husband and dad, a considerate son, a game player, a writer, and an incredible trainer. Each of those worlds is a game that Ronen plays and in which he therefore aims to win. Some of Simcha's multiple dimensions include being a musician, a snowboarder, a pet owner of Arnie the rabbit, a great husband and dad, a helpful sibling, an engaging speaker, and a TRXer. Each of those worlds is a game that Simcha plays and in which he therefore aims to win.

Each dimension is meaningful in its own way as well as challenging, fun, inspiring, and an integrated part of reality. None of these dimensions is dependent on the currency of money for its inherent value. In other words, you don't have to be able to monetize everything you do for it to be something valuable that serves you in your life. This is the beauty of being multidimensional New Entrepreneurz celebrating all the different aspects of who they are. Each dimension allows us to step proudly forward and find self-expression and joy when we play the games that we play. Smartly.

If you love what you do and do what you love, that's the best. Who cares if others do more, bigger, louder, or differently? They're just playing different games, and in the same way that they can be winners in their games, you can be a winner in yours, too. Being a winner doesn't imply being exclusive. If there's room for collaboration, collaborate! We believe people are powerful, have integrity, and want to grow and develop themselves. Just by picking up this book you are already on the New Entrepreneurz path. Let's expand the number of possible ways each of us can win our own game! Ready to expand? Here goes.

## FreshBiziology 101: The Language and Mind-Set

- *Win to the Winth Power*—Win-win is so last year. Win to the Winth Power is multidimensional winning, the type that is collaborative and expansive and creates winning in many dimensions with many people simultaneously.

- *Action Cards*—Nonmonetary currency composed of all your unique gifts that can be leveraged to move you and others forward in life. From your skills and abilities to your knowledge base and your connections, this is the currency of the New Entrepreneurz.

- *Throw the Dice*—Taking action is how you collaborate with the universe. You make a move, and it makes a move. If ever you find yourself stuck, just throw the dice. The good news is that you can throw as many as you'd like.

- *Zoom Out*—Pause, breathe, and look out from being in the thick of things to widen your view, broaden your perspective, and take a holistic look at the total picture. This allows people to see more opportunities and possibilities than what was there previously.

- *Quantum Leap*—An incredible new reality that comes about without the typical planned, linear progress. One minute you are here, and the next minute you are all the way over there, celebrating the miracle!

- *Red Titles and Green Titles*—Our perspective on what we see as mandatory (red titles) versus optional (green titles). Red titles are things that we must or must not do rather than things we may choose or choose not to do.

- *Smartnership*—Smart partnerships created strategically to bring everyone success, results, and winning through providing tremendous value all around.

- *Smarketing*—Smart marketing where instead of selling, pitching, convincing, or recruiting, you simply share your unique message the right way and attract your ideal customers or community to you, with ease.

- *Internpreneur*—The new type of interns, the type who don't just make you coffee, await you babysitting them, and wait *in turn* for instructions. These Millennials are creative and proactive and can really make a difference in your company—if you just get out of the way and let them.

- *Communitycation*—Communicating directly with your community. When engaged in the same mind-set rhythm as others around you, your communication and community become transformational.

# 1 Ronen Tells the Story behind FreshBiz

*The value of an idea lies in the using of it.*

—Thomas Edison

**Figure 1.1**   Or Kaplan

From a very young age I sensed, and later realized, that the games that we are all taught to play in life might not be the right ones, not for me personally, and maybe not for the world either.

School was the perfect example of my dichotomy. Inherently feeling that society was playing the wrong game of education, I never cared much about grades and was willing to invest time and effort only in those subjects that fascinated me. Even then, my goal was never to achieve good grades. Seeking the rationale behind the curriculum subjects, I was disappointed repeatedly when teachers couldn't adequately address that question. Clearly, learning more about topics that specifically interested me meant looking for more information myself. Before you shrug, smile, and think to yourself, "Well, there's the Internet . . . " keep in mind that the Internet didn't make its big splash into our lives until some 20 years later, so my only option was combing library after library, searching in physical books.

A question that puzzled me endlessly was *why* we need to learn the things we were being taught. Simply put: Why should we study math, physics, literature, and music, and how might they integrate into new holistic understandings and not just fields of accrued knowledge? But that's the structure of the game of formal education, which focuses chiefly on gaining knowledge for the sake of knowledge rather than developing new insights or creative thinking.

Having said that, there *was* one school subject I loved: economics! I could get the logic of it, the interaction between cause and effect and its application to real life.

It was fascinating, and I wanted to know more about the world of business, which gave the impression of being one tremendous, compelling game.

Books, books, and more books absorbed me totally, especially the narratives about what would later be called multinational or global companies, such as Coca-Cola, McDonald's, Microsoft, and others, and their founders. I was always amazed by the mind-set that enabled people to develop such huge companies more than the companies themselves. It wasn't the money, the sales, or the market value of those companies that grabbed my attention most; it was what it took to make big dreams come true.

Let's backtrack for a moment to my early years. Because I was born with a heart defect, much of my early childhood was spent in hospitals, undergoing major surgery at four years old and later needing to cope with numerous related health issues. They were all encapsulated in childhood memories as images of hospitals and a series of unpleasant experiences. Years later, a physician supervising my annual checkup expressed amazement that I was still around.

That made me wonder if a guardian angel hadn't given me a second chance, and if so, then the only and obvious conclusion was that I should do something meaningful with my life. My parents, on the other hand, had a different approach. Not wanting anything worse to happen to me, they felt that resting was vital. The upshot of their under-standable concern was an overprotected childhood. But the downside of being protected against bad stuff happening is that not much life happens either.

There would be no going on school trips, sleeping over at friends' houses, or playing group sports, and it wasn't uncommon when I did leave the house to hear one of my parents yell out, "Remember, life is already challenging enough. You don't need to go looking for more trouble." I truly appreciate my parents' situation and am immensely grateful for their love and support, but keeping me from life was tough. Because we have the choice, however, of focusing on the positive aspect of any situation, I can definitely say that three good things surfaced from that period:

1. Because I wasn't out there with my peers as much as I wanted, I got to spend a lot of time getting ready for the rest of my life.
2. I developed a deep understanding of what it means to try to prevent life from happening, which I eventually realized is something many people do every day out of fear.
3. I came to see that life really is a game. As long as we're healthy, everything else is no more than mind games. In actuality, health, too, can be viewed as a type of a mind game.

My specific circumstances led to the realization that playing the wrong games in life would be a waste of effort, and effort involves time. So what games *were* people playing, and what would classify them as good?

Like my peers, upon completing high school I enlisted for military service in the Israel Defense Forces, but because of my health status, I earned an immediate exemption from any combat unit. Wanting to contribute what I could to the State of Israel and the security of its people, I enlisted in the capacity of computer programmer for the mandatory three years. Free time in the afternoons was an opportunity to become certified as a stock broker, along with my best friend at the time. We jumped into the deep end of the stock market game.

Although we were just two regular draftees with a monthly paycheck of about $100 each, with some great connections and neat negotiation skills, we swung about $100,000 in credit from the bank! It was crazy, and we had a good deal of fun playing the stock market. There were days when we made $300 to $500, which we thought was awesome compared to our salaries. We enjoyed playing around with our big earnings, but we also learned some very valuable lessons along the way:

1. The stock market is a game of skills. Invest time and effort in suitable education, and you can create great wins.

2. Money is a game. Win some; lose some. Either way, the experiences and anecdotes remain yours forever.

3. You don't need huge earnings to have fun; you just need to know how to put what you have to good use. Believe me; we had some unforgettable vacations with those $300 earnings.

About three months before my military service was due to end, the Israeli stock market not only caved, but in retrospect, it also turned out to be the greatest collapse in its entire history. What perfect timing. As I stepped back into civilian life, I started out with a gift of about $10,000 in debt.

It was pretty shocking at the time, but I recall constantly comforting myself with a simple sentence: "It's just a game of win some, lose some, and one day it'll be summarized as one line in a book." So here it is: I lost $10,000 in the stock market!

Over the years that followed, I moved into the business game through several initiatives in the StartupNation, learning about programming, sales, marketing, service, accounting, money, and many other aspects of running a business. Formal higher education was struck off my list altogether after the third time I quit college: It was so much more thrilling to spend my time doing rather than sitting in the classroom talking about what can theoretically be done. The straw that broke the camel's back and led me to realize just how much college life was not what I wanted was when I left one of my final exams an hour before the allocated time, without finishing the exam, because it conflicted with a business meeting I really wanted to be at.

Don't get me wrong: I'm not saying that higher education is irrelevant or has no purpose, but it wasn't the right game for me. With hindsight, I also believe it's not the right game for many people who are still playing it, but they remain unaware of this because they never stop to check thoroughly. In my case, however, the more games I got the chance to play in life, the more I realized what was, and what wasn't, working for me.

At the age of 30, I realized that being a salaried employee was too slow and unfulfilling for me, so I chose to quit my job and become an entrepreneur—or in other words, be unemployed! Although at this point I was married and had a three-year-old boy, I needed greater freedom to implement the dream of being my own boss. There was one hitch to this grand concept: I had no clear idea of what my dreams actually were or how to go about making them come true. But I did know that I needed to do things differently. That's when I flitted from one venture to another in the world of software and Web development. Simultaneously, I signed up for the most expensive higher education program there is: the university of life.

A year later my wife, Anat, and I bought a house and a mortgage and moved to a location about 40 minutes north of Tel Aviv. This seemed to me the most obvious and perfect time to come to my wife and present an idea. I suggested that instead of only me not making any money, we could both not make money together. Anat is one of the most talented graphic designers I know, so we decided on a boutique branding agency. She'd be in charge of design, while my skills would cover marketing and sales. Anat's "yes" led to our own family business, the boutique branding agency we called Fresh.

Our entrance into the world of entrepreneurship was a huge leap of faith because we had nothing and no one to fall back on should the business not succeed. We defined success simply: producing enough income to repay the mortgage and cover basic living costs.

What made us go for it, despite the fears and risks, was the fact that we saw this as a step in the right direction toward greater self-expression for us both. It was a move, we knew, that would make us grow as people, as a couple, and as professionals. It was appealing: an exciting challenge.

Actually, our mutual agreement to take this path wasn't a complete surprise. Anat and I met each other at a self-development seminar; she was actually my coach, so from the start our thoughts about personal growth as a main life goal were in alignment. Jim Rohn says it best: "Don't wish it was easier; wish you were better."

Was there a price to pay for making this move? Of course, but it was one we were willing to pay. There were some people who made it clear to us that they thought our venture was irresponsible. On the other hand, we considered foregoing our dreams as irresponsible. Because I was such a "successful" entrepreneur at that point, we set out on this adventure with a net worth of about $100,000 in debt! Here's a thought to consider: If you're starting out right now with nothing, you're already $100,000 ahead of where we were.

Around that time, the aha! moment came in the form of an insight. I wanted to show people that the game of business could be played in ways other than those to which they'd become accustomed. I wanted people to realize that business didn't have to focus on who makes the most money but could be a much more expansive, fulfilling, and awesome game if they changed their approach and mind-set.

On a mild October night in 2003, I found myself sitting in the yard, writing down all the ideas and concepts for the board game. FreshBiz was born.

I couldn't configure the fine details of the whole picture back then, but now, 10 years later, I see that the game's basic elements were already clearly outlined. What I *was* certain of was that the game had to be completely new, nothing like any other game that had been played before. It had to take people through the challenges and excitement of being an entrepreneur. More accurately, it had to lead each player into becoming an entrepreneurial thinker.

I knew that our new branding business could be successful because I'd gained an understanding on how to turn debt into opportunity. I knew that given sufficient time, I could turn things around, overcome the challenges and obstacles, and be a winner.

*That* was precisely what the game should contain.

In retrospect, that's when the realization clinched about the life games I'd played so far and didn't enjoy, whether they were called education, business, and relationships or Monopoly, bridge, and chess. They were all fear-based games, and the fear was of losing because losing was a negative. To not lose, one had to win. To win, competition was deemed essential. In the world of gaming, this type of zero-sum game is known as last man standing. This means that to be the ultimate winner, everyone else has to lose. What a horrible way to train children who later become adults!

How do students win at school? Simple, by getting higher marks than other students. Is there any motivation for collaboration in that system? No, none at all. How do you win at college or university? Simple, by getting a great job. Any collaboration there? No. If you don't find that great job, and you have no money, well, it's game over for you, right?

From childhood on, we've been trained to think that a healthy business can function only in a state of competition. We're sold, even brainwashed, to believe that success means killing the competitor and dominating the market. Actually, none of that is true, and this book will explain why in more detail.

Even relationships have been tainted by this prevalent competitive approach. I've seen many couples keep a running scoreboard on who is a better parent, trying to get more points from simple household chores, such as doing the laundry, to activities that shouldn't even be considered a chore, such as spending quality time with the kids.

Then there's the scariest game of all—the money game. Layer upon layer of fear drives it. Have any of these thoughts ever entered your head? *Wow, what if we won't have enough money for food? What does it say about me if I have less than others? How can I risk leaving my job and ending up poorer?* Also, have you noticed that when talking about money the tone of the conversation suddenly changes? That's because people are trying to keep track of the rules they've been told are vital to the money game: Don't share how much you make, don't give any information away, and keep your cards close to your chest.

Think about this: There are so many limiting beliefs and fears about money that too often they either drive us crazy or make us freeze and be incapable of breaking loose. In the game I was outlining that evening in the garden, I wanted to present an alternative to those fears, I wanted to present the dimension of money as only one of many dimensions, and I wanted people to understand that business and even life itself are not competition-based games at all. It was important to me that the game reach its end because of a restricted time frame and *not* because one player beat out all the others.

So FreshBiz became a time-limited game, with money as a means but absolutely not a goal, just like life!

What else did I want for this game? The opportunity to celebrate divergent and entrepreneurial thinking. I wanted people to enjoy the freedom of flexible, unusual, unexpected, or alternative choices rather than following a set of instructions. College should be a choice, not a requirement. A salaried job, or getting married, should be choices, not requirements. That's how I came up with the game's red and green titles explained in greater detail later in the book.

Constantly I returned to the guiding principle that life is not a one-dimensional game. It's multidimensional, just as people are: Each of us *plays multiple roles* and has multiple talents. FreshBiz was founded as a multidimensional game where you, the player, get to play any or all of them at any given time as a way of expressing yourself, limited only by your creativity.

I wanted to present people with opportunities and the ability to see those opportunities all around them. This concept manifests in the game as Action Cards, which you can learn to leverage as additional alternative currencies that are often worth way more than just money. Then the idea that you can't move forward in life because of insufficient funds would just dissolve away.

Developing FreshBiz was exciting and challenging. It took me six years and involved partnering and unpartnering, major investments of time and money, and facing inner fears and the complexities arising from simultaneously building up two businesses, the game, and the branding studio while building my healthy family. It involved reinforcing my own self-development, self-expression, and self-confidence. Together, Anat and I also learned to overcome relationship issues, and those were some tricky times. But all in all, it was great for building character and creating muscle memory in turning our ideas into reality together.

By the time the game was ready to take to the next level, we were left with one big hurdle to overcome: We still had a $100,000 debt. By putting all the elements of the game into practice in our real lives, we turned the branding studio into a success, and it provided for our family during those several years while I was developing the FreshBiz game. But because I'd needed to invest a lot of money in game development, and because it took a while for the studio to become profitable, we never managed to save enough to repay the debt.

Then the moment came to turn the game into a business.

Wanting initially to maintain my creative freedom in structuring the business in the spirit of the game, I opted for avoiding investors. But the need for a decision that would address the question of "What do we do next?" made us take a good look at our Action Cards, and we spotted a big one: our house. Yes, the one we'd bought six years earlier. Luckily the real estate market was thriving, and our house was worth about $150,000 more than what we'd paid.

There were two choices open to us. One was to let go of the house: sell it, pay back the debt, and be left with something to invest in the business. The second option was to keep the house, keep the debt, find an alternative way to cover the loans, and find investment funds for the business.

With our options under the proverbial magnifying glass, we saw this: Letting go of the house meant letting go of old beliefs and fears about the idea that "Not owning a house is not as good as owning a house." We embarked on an important process of reframing our concepts around dreams, fulfillment, happiness, risks, and home. Ultimately, we chose to sell the house, pay back the debt, and invest in FreshBiz.

What helped make the decision easier for us (and trust me; it wasn't a smile, wink, and shrug kind of decision by any means!) were two fundamental concepts we shared:

1. Home is not a house. Home is where you get to live your full potential, and it has nothing to do with finances or ownership.

2. Because either option presents prices to pay and risks to take, the bottom line is, will our decision be based on the fear of losing or the excitement of success?

If you're reading this book, you already know what we chose. Excitement, baby!

Incidentally, moving day came much later than we'd ever imagined. For their own personal reasons, our buyers didn't want to move into the house until two years later, so we paid them rent and stayed where we were.

Our new reality now looked like this: same house, same monthly payment but diverted to rent instead of mortgage, no debt, and bingo—$100,000 for investment in FreshBiz!

Looking back, we made a smart business decision. The price of the house rose since then by $100,000 more, but the investment in FreshBiz turned into a few million dollars in company evaluation, dreams coming true, visiting incredible countries, and changing people's lives for the better. Not a bad deal at all. But we didn't have to wait to discover we were winners. We knew we'd already won the game from the moment we sold the house. How did we know that? You can read all about it in the chapter titled, "Teaser: You've Already Won the Game."

Making this move created the opportunity for turning FreshBiz from a sidekick venture into a business, and since that day back in 2010, we've been on a fun, challenging, crazy, fulfilling ride.

Along the way I also got lucky, meeting incredible people who joined the journey. Two of them are Simcha Gluck, who's cowriting this book, and Joshua Weiss. Both later became my founding partners in FreshBiz. Many other talented individuals have become our business centers, managers, or facilitators around the globe.

We are true believers in building smart businesses rather than big businesses. We believe in seeking quality rather than quantity. We describe that approach in the chapters titled "Win to the Winth Power" and "Smart Business." These philosophies helped us create a lean and smart business, allowing us the lifestyle we always wanted in which we get to be game changers, world travelers, and Life Hackers (explained in Chapter 2) while spending quality time with our families.

FreshBiz is now global, through workshops run for tens of thousands of people in more than 20 countries. In this book we share with you some of the stories from our travels, such as how we ended up in front of 50 million viewers in India and how the students at Indian Institute of Technology Bombay reacted to a lifestyle challenge and how, using our Win-to-the-Winth-Power approach, we solved a problem that surfaced unexpectedly in Russia.

I sincerely believe that becoming a New Entrepreneur is possible for anyone willing to learn the basic concepts and put them into action. I've coached multitudes of people, and it's clear without any doubt that winning the game is no more than a matter of being willing to invest in your personal growth and then doing something different in your life with what you learned.

I also sincerely believe that we can better this world we live in if we play with Win-to-the-Winth-Power thinking instead of competing with each other. I believe that we can achieve a more enriching balance of our lives' diverse dimensions and that education can be aimed at creativity and self-development instead of turning out worker bees for the workforce. I'm sure there are people who think I'm too naïve, but because we're almost at the end of this chapter and you're still with us, I guess it means you too are part of what we like to call the tribe of the New Entrepreneurz.

Becoming a New Entrepreneur starts as an inner process and then moves outward, which is why I invite you not just to read the book but also to engage in the game outside the book that we talk about in the chapter titled "What Game Are You Playing?"

So play life, and live big.

Oh, and we recently bought a new house!

# 2 The New Entrepreneurz

*All humans are entrepreneurs not because they should start companies but because the will to create is encoded in human DNA.*

—Reid Hoffman, LinkedIn cofounder

**Figure 2.1**   Josh Zlotnick

When we write the New Entrepreneurz with a *z* at the end, we refer to the specific group of New Entrepreneurz who are also FreshBizers, the ones who play life with a Win-to-the-Winth-Power mind-set. These are the ones who flick their magic wands to expand life, innovate seamlessly, create quantum leaps, and even have an air of serious playfulness as they do it. They make running organizations, businesses, and charities look and feel fun! Jon Vroman is a perfect example with the way he runs the Front Row Foundation. (Learn more about him in the Interviews section at the back of the book.) He's a New Entrepreneur with the passionate belief that everyone should be living life as a participant in the front row, rather than as a spectator in the back row, and this is exactly the experience that recipients of the Front Row Foundation's services get. The foundation gives amazing people, many with terminal illnesses, and their families a front row seat at the concert or sporting event of their dreams. Aside from this being a magic moment, the foundation continues making a difference through coaching, support, and celebrating life with the families for years to come.

Let's reflect for a moment on the New Entrepreneurz, who they are, who they're not, and what is so different about them that we felt compelled to add the word *New* to their title. Here's the in-a-nutshell way of looking at business evolution and entrepreneurship in the twentieth century.

## First, a Brief History Lesson

The rat race was born from the Industrial Revolution's factory mind-set. Essentially, the harder we work, the more products

come off the conveyor belt at the end of the day, and ultimately, the more money the factory makes. People were just
human machines working in deplorable conditions. Factory
owners maximized profits by paying people as little as possible to work for as long and as quickly as possible. Money was
perceived as an important but scarce commodity. In the cycli-
cal agricultural world before the Industrial Revolution, food
and income were linked to unreliable seasons, but factories
offered stable income.

Initially, workers were excited to start work as early they
could, stay as late as they could, and take minimal bath-
room and meal breaks to maximize their earnings. They were
thrilled that money could be earned throughout the year,
independent of seasonality. People began extolling the virtues
of hard work and the serious worker who is so committed that
he or she doesn't have time even to think about a vacation.
That gave rise to this mind-set: If you're not a hard worker,
you're a lazy good-for-nothing.

The Great Depression of 1929 shook the confidence of
the business world when the stock market collapsed, along
with many businesses. People learned a lesson: It's risky to be
a business owner and shoulder so much responsibility. There
were no quick, cheap, and easy Internet tools like there are
nowadays. So the masses learned to play it safe by becoming
employees and looking for jobs with business owners or corporations powerful enough to shield them from a fall in case
of another Great Depression.

Employees believed jobs were a safety net offering
security, and they worked hard, dedicating hours for the sake

of security and a weekly paycheck. Employee loyalty was rewarded and working for the same company for decades was considered perfectly normal. Many people literally began in the mailrooms and, through dedication, worked their way to higher positions and pay grades over the course of years on their way to retirement at age 65 or 67.

All of that created the mind-set of working hard and playing it safe.

Jumping forward a few decades to when the Internet took off, you no longer needed a brick-and-mortar business to be considered a business owner. Now you could have a business that functions in a place called cyberspace, where the only amount of money you pay for real estate is the price of your domain name plus hosting. Barriers to becoming a successful business owner were almost entirely destroyed as brick and mortar switched into click and order. E-commerce was the fastest-growing area, and search tools got exponentially better, aided by social media, which took branding, messaging, and engagement into a whole new stratosphere. More and more people began waking up to their entrepreneurial calling, leveraging these new tools for their own success.

However, although technology has changed, the mainstream mind-set has primarily stayed the same.

## The Lone Worker

Entrepreneurs began breaking free of the system years ago. Many of the entrepreneurs we meet in our FreshBiz workshops tell us how much they love the freedom to do what they're doing and to pursue things their way. They view their business as one of the most fulfilling forms of self-expression and are excited and passionate about it. Every time we hear that, we think of the famous quote, "Follow your dreams, or you'll spend the rest of your life working for someone who did."

Entrepreneurs began blazing their own trails as they pursued their dreams. Soon, many became Lone Workers. This reminds us of Simcha's grandfather, who had his own candy shop on the Lower East Side of Manhattan, or our friend who sells cool and funky hair accessories through her website. Although the success and profits are theirs and theirs alone to keep, Lone Workers have substantially less of everything needed to grow their business. Because most small business owners tend to view themselves as big businesses in micro, they often find themselves stuck.

It ends up being ironic that Lone Workers who left the corporate world because they didn't like working 9 AM to 5 PM now find themselves working 5 AM to 9 PM because they don't have a team or departments to assist them. The Lone Workers who didn't want to be employees for someone else are now employees for themselves but without all the resources. There's no marketing department, accounting division, customer service center, and so on. Essentially, whatever they're working on at any moment in time is what's going on in their business. With an online business, online tools help give them some of the support they so desperately need, but for the barber in his own barbershop or Simcha's grandfather in his candy shop—it's all on them and them alone. They really deserve praise for their courage and strength!

## Simcha's Marketing Company

My wife, Rachel, and I jumped at the opportunity to run the New York City district office for a large marketing company after spending a couple of years working together as sales reps and graduating from Queens College. We were young, struggling newlyweds right after graduation when we finally found where we wanted to set up shop. It was a cute little place along the Long Island Expressway, close to a cemetery and a 7-Eleven. To save on expenses we decided against a storefront location, realizing that we'd be creating our own people traffic anyway. We spent a small fortune paying the first several months of rent up front; buying, finding, and setting up our office furnishings; getting the business phone lines up and running; hiring receptionists; and managing to keep some liquidity to help us float the first few months. We knew those months might mean no income. It was a challenge that almost ripped my marriage to pieces, too!

Running this business was like spinning plates and juggling hundreds of balls constantly. This is how it worked: If I didn't spend time on advertising, then no advertising happened that week. Driving receptionist productivity was necessary, but that meant I wasn't driving sales productivity. Driving sales productivity was great, but I couldn't simultaneously drive advertising activity. It was a perpetual game of Whack-a-Mole: Just as you finish smashing one mole with your bopper, two or three more quickly pop out of their holes. A manager in a different territory said it best: "You learn to live with the fact that even when you're making great money, your office will still feel chaotic and you'll feel like a failure daily."

It was exhausting trying to give the different areas of my business the love and finesse that only I could give. At first, Rachel and I didn't have the right people to delegate things to, and eventually when we did, they just never gave it the love that we would give it. I dropped the ball constantly, not because I was an irresponsible person, but because there were just too many balls in the air at the same time, with only two hands at my disposal. The trophies, bonus checks, and paid vacations that we got for hitting different sales goals were like an awesome orange carrot dangled in front of us that kept us going. But it sure as hell couldn't replace our dizzying exhaustion.

Although we all worked very hard, to this day that period remains one of the greatest experiences because I learned that my capacity is above and beyond what I ever thought possible. It planted within me seeds of greatness, and to this day I'm still friends with many of the managers and sales leaders from the company, all of whom are exceptional people. Looking back at it now, knowing what I know about the New Entrepreneurz and building smart businesses, I now understand what a difference it makes to work smart rather than work hard.

## Strength and Courage

The Lone Workers are amazingly brave people. When you walk along the main street in your community, typically the stores and eateries are just the periphery on your stroll. But did you ever stop to think that behind any shop's opening and closing is someone's daughter, son, uncle, or loved one who's just lost tens if not hundreds of thousands of dollars?

In the beginning, we're all so proud of our friend for starting that diner or opening a car wash. It's the American Dream being realized! But there can be a lot of pain in those hours of no customers, dwindling resources, and equipment not holding up. The Lone Workers deserve a big hug for the courage and strength that woke them at the crack of dawn so that they could invest their passion in serving you to make your life better.

The problem with this model is that many Lone Workers who lived the dream of working for themselves reached retirement with no pension or ability to retire. The younger generation saw the dilemma: the unappealing option of being an employee for 40 years or the equally unappealing choice of being the Lone Worker for 40 years with daily roller coasters in their business and no financial security to show for it.

## Introducing: The Lifestyle Entrepreneur

The next phase of entrepreneurship is the Lifestyle Entrepreneur. Whereas Lone Workers were engaged in their own type of rat race, aiming to retire eventually from the hard work of running their own business, the Lifestyle Entrepreneurs want to work harder when young so that they can retire much earlier. They focus on being active now to produce passive income later that releases them from office drudgery. The idea is never to work again and instead to enjoy a lifestyle of endless five-star vacations with other rich and famous people. Robert Kiyosaki, in his book *Rich Dad, Poor Dad,* calls this "having money work for you instead of you working for money." This mantra drives these entrepreneurs to work hard now for a lifetime of indulgent laziness later. Imagine you created the E-ZPass system used for bridges and tunnels in the northeastern region of the United States, and now every time a car drives through, you get a few cents put right into your bank account, no matter where you are.

Here are some of the most popular paths taken by Lifestyle Entrepreneurs of the past few decades:

- Investing in real estate
- Investing in the stock market
- Writing self-help books/e-books
- Becoming a network marketer
- Becoming an affiliate marketer

The concept behind all these paths is great. Leverage always works when done the right way. But for many people the dream of passive income rolling in so that they can *really* enjoy their lives stays just that: a dream. Whether you're flipping foreclosures, selling a stock short, penning that nonfiction, promoting a new health product, or building the right team—it takes energy, and achieving success in any of the options listed means being very smart and executing the right moves.

It's not as simple as just taking a $5,000 course, learning the seven magic secrets, or reading a few books on the topic. It takes time, energy, and practice to succeed in these areas and create mastery. Above and beyond all else, it takes the right mind-set. We're definitely not saying these areas aren't worth your effort, but if you choose this path, do so with your eyes wide open.

## Take the *Lie* out of Lifestyle—and Put *Life* Back In

We're strong believers in leverage and working smart. What we're not keen on when it comes to passive income is the way it's usually presented. Trust us; we've been there, from stock markets to network marketing to real estate investments. Once-in-a-lifetime opportunities are too often presented as get-rich-quick programs. You hear the stories and see the images: vacations, sports cars, big houses, and shiny rewards. We believe those stories and images are delivering the wrong message. They're working like the dangled carrot that keeps you going through the hard days and nights of presentations, talks, events, losses, paperwork, or whatever is needed to make it in those businesses.

They sell you on the lifestyle *moments* and not on the lifestyle itself.

Real estate investment can be great: exploring the country looking for deals, working the numbers, renovating houses, and offering new value. Network marketing can be a great way to go if you find a quality product and like to build teams and coach people, but those actions should be taken because you want to add value to your life through day-to-day activities and challenges, not because it's something you have to get through to enjoy some lifestyle later at the end of the rainbow.

For some people these are great opportunities and can make for a good lifestyle, but for the New Entrepreneurz this is not enough.

## The New Entrepreneurz

Instead of trying to squeeze lifestyle into a break, a vacation, or a Sunday afternoon, the New Entrepreneurz simply design a life framework with their desired lifestyle already built in. This group sees business and productivity itself as a lifestyle, where every day of the journey is challenging, fulfilling, and fun, just like the lifestyle they thrive on. They don't want the game to end when they're 40, 50, or 60. Why would they? Nor do they see retirement as moving to a tropical island where they'll drink margaritas alone or with a small elite group every day. That's just not their aspiration.

Instead, this new breed of entrepreneurs are game changers. What makes them different is their attitude about who they are and why they're doing what they do. Take Hickies for example: an incredible company, founded by a great couple, Gaston Frydlewski and Mariquel Waingarten, as a way to spend more time together while spreading love and positivity through an innovative, fun, and fashionable replacement for shoelaces. (Learn more about Mariquel in the Interviews section at the back of the book.)

The New Entrepreneurz are purpose driven, strong believers in smart work, and great collaborators. They understand that life is happening right now, and if it's right now, then they're also going to have some fun and create some memories along the way!

## The Life Hackers and Gamers

*You never change things by fighting the existing reality. To change something, build a new model that makes the existing model obsolete.*

—Bucky Fuller

The New Entrepreneurz see life as a game. They're not afraid of or overwhelmed by playing simultaneous games. Actually, they love doing that. By gamers we don't mean 8 hours a day on Second Life or playing Xbox and Playstation. The Life Hackers and Gamers we refer to step into different roles and wear different hats in real life. Instead of feeling scattered, with too many things going on, they embrace multiplicity as the mark of a healthy multidimensional human being just playing numerous games. As multidimensional thinkers, they find joy in connecting the different dots that make up their lives.

Nowadays, we all multitask. It's part of our new nature that we adopt varied roles in varied shows every day. We get to play parents, kids, business owners, partners, cooks, musicians, and more. Although it could be exhausting, and we sometimes hear the older generations complaining about that, the New Entrepreneurz don't see it that way. They choose a different mind-set. Instead of battling the variety, they embrace it and have fun with it, knowing it's what makes people so unique and special. In the words of William Cowper, "Variety is the very spice of life that gives it all its flavor."

If you've ever come across the problem of what to put on your business card or what to enter as your LinkedIn profile

**Figure 2.2**　Alyssa Faith Weiss

title because no single word captures all your passions, then you know exactly what we're talking about. Just think of how many people are now using the | to separate yet present all their different hats at once, for example: Author | Trainer | Consultant | Speaker.

For too long we were told, "Pick one," "Focus," "Stop being all over the place," "Get a solid profession," "Specialize," along with other old-school beliefs on how to live, work, and present ourselves to the world. That might have even been good advice once upon a time, but that time is over. When we meet someone new, there's the usual question of "What do you do?" The answer always goes something like this: "Well . . . first we developed this game; then workshops were created around it, and now we visit countries, training top people and companies. Oh, and we're also authors . . ." You get the point.

There's no single title that covers all those activities, and there doesn't have to be. Likewise, it's okay if you cannot explain everything you do in a 20-second elevator pitch to the Shark Tank. Too often in the world of entrepreneurship, so much time and energy is focused on the pitch and having to nail every aspect of who you are and what you do in a matter of seconds. We've created so much fear and pressure around entrepreneurs needing to be able to give over their entire identity in less than a minute. But that doesn't work for many people, and it shouldn't have to. Learn to give over your message powerfully and that if you have something valuable to say or offer, trust that the right people will hear. By the way, when was the last time you met an investor in an elevator and had only 20 seconds to talk to him or her?

We're multigamers, simultaneously being inventors, marketers, coaches, parents, and friends, and we don't really want to separate the games into parts. This is actually one of the reasons why women make some of the best New Entrepreneurz, because of their incredible knack for multitasking and doing it with love.

We aim to improve how we play our games and possibly add some new ones. We're not looking to retire at some fixed age the way Lone Workers did. But we're also not looking to stop our games early like Lifestyle Entrepreneurs. We don't want to be labeled, either. Titles such as chief executive officer (CEO), marketing manager, and author don't cut it anymore. Try putting "Life Hacker and Gamer" on your business card. That will surely be a conversation starter! It'll let you talk about the different games you play in life and allow you to invite fresh new players to your table to play with.

Here's a story of a Life Hacker, someone who plays many games in life and is an awesome human being as well. We met Professor Bruce Bachenheimer when we prelaunched the FreshBiz workshops in New York City and one of our partners had set up a morning meeting for us. (Learn more about Bruce in the Interviews section at the end of the book.) It was an unforgettable day because it was the same day as our first ever FreshBiz workshop in New York City. It was held at a shared workspace in downtown Manhattan called Hive at 55 and was so new that only 16 people had registered for an event meant for double that amount. Right before the meeting with Bruce, we were discussing how to generate the quantum leap needed for a full house. So we did what we always do; we rolled the dice and took action!

The meeting with Bruce turned out to be amazing. We shared stories about the StartupNation, the Entrepreneurship Lab at Pace University, and the FreshBiz game, which he absolutely loved. Acknowledging that it was a last-minute invitation, we invited him to join our evening event. We were hoping if he attended that we'd have at least one more quality participant, not to mention we might gain a potential foot in the door of one of New York's finest universities. Bruce mentally checked his schedule and advised that unfortunately the workshop coincided with a teaching session. Then he paused, smiled broadly, and said, "Why don't I just bring the entire class over on a field trip? It *is* the entrepreneurship class, afterall."

Just like that, at 7:15 PM, Bruce and 15 students strode through the door and turned the workshop into a packed event, making for great pictures, great stories, and valuable connections. In that moment we knew we'd met a professor who plays a different type of game, and it reinforced the power of what we talk about in our workshops: The only way to achieve a quantum leap is to see opportunities and take action. To go from half-full to full through taking just one action, our meeting, was extraordinary!

For our next trip to the United States, Bruce set us up with a workshop for nearly 100 Pace University students and professors. It was a massive success and led to Bruce sharing more of his personal story.

Bruce started out as a successful Wall Street trader. He remembers the first time he did a trade for a billion dollars in one clip. Everyone viewed him as hugely successful. The sensible thing for him to do would have been to continue making money on Wall Street and live the American Dream. But Bruce, an entrepreneurial thinker, had other plans. Reading *Walden; or, Life in the Woods* by Henry David Thoreau led him to realize how uninspired he was. He felt that doing more of the same for money and prestige lacked purpose and pleasure. He left his job, bought a boat, learned to sail, and spent the next seven years sailing. He even named his 36-foot yacht *Deliberate* from a passage in Thoreau's book. It was his reminder always to live life deliberately, with choice, power, and conviction.

Bruce wore multiple hats during this period: stockbroker and sailor. But upon coming back to land, he learned to be a woodworker, opened a few businesses, and then became a professor, opening Pace University's Entrepreneurship Lab. He explained to us how much he loves living the type of life where anything could happen next. This is exactly what we mean by New Entrepreneurz, Life Hackers, and Gamers who play multiple games. We'd love to see more professors like Bruce inspiring students and entrepreneurs through their real-life know-how and not just through classroom knowledge.

Bruce's poem, which he kindly shared with us, encapsulates his journey of leaving everything behind to set sail and live his dreams.

### Deliberate

I went to the sea to live deliberately
Abandoning this harried life which somehow seduced me
Knowing that harsh reality would constantly challenge me
Liberating the fleeting spirit buried deep within me

Longing to see the works of the Lord

Quietly deliberating dreams from vain desires coerced subliminally

I must go down to the sea today

Before these dreams and I quietly fade away

Prof. Bruce Bachenheimer, Clinical Professor of Management, Pace U. | Director, Entrepreneurship Lab | Sailor | Poet

## The Social Gamers and Global Thinkers

Many of the New Entrepreneurz we meet at our events run smart, lean businesses right from their laptops, smartphones, and tablets. Needing nothing more than a Wi-Fi connection, they're free to live wherever they like with other fun people of the same mind-set.

The New Entrepreneurz don't see why they should be stuck in a polluted, rainy city when they could be on the beach in Thailand, Bali, or Hawaii. We hear this rhetorical question all the time from New Entrepreneurz participating in programs such as the Tropical MBA, Project Getaway, or NomadicHUB, which are among the incredible programs for entrepreneurial communities that want to enjoy a fun life while building purpose-driven businesses remotely.

Now more than ever before, you can run a business with greater freedom and flexibility. If spiriting yourself away to a tropical island is a bit too bold for you at the moment, or you don't want to take your kids out of school (which we can understand), there are still great ways to build your own unique supporting working environment where you live. We meet hundreds of entrepreneurs all over the globe, working from coffee shops, rooftops, gardens, or shared workspaces with other like-minded people in their cities. Once you break out from the office cubicle and make sure you have a Wi-Fi connection, the sky's the limit, so fly free!

New Entrepreneurz also understand that playing and winning works better in a team than alone. Teaming up used to work only if you were in a company or part of a college system. All those Lone Worker entrepreneurs walked a lonely path, knowing they had to make it on their own with no one helping them win the game. Nowadays you can be part of a team even when you're the only employee in your business. Just look at the GameChangers 500 (a special list of companies we'll explain more later in the chapter) company known as Achievers, which created a brilliant software system that makes it easy for people to recognize and reward each other's successes even across different companies. You can join Facebook and LinkedIn groups, go to Meetups, log in to forums, and plug in to coworking spaces as an entrepreneur to play as a team.

A shift in mind-set drove technology to make these tools and locations available. As social creatures, we love to share, work, and play together. But for centuries we were indoctrinated with rules of competition, so that's how we played. Modern technology and social media now let us go back to our true sharing nature, and it is refreshing.

New Entrepreneurz understand the power of sharing: They share information, knowledge, experiences, connections, opportunities, and Action Cards. They play a global game of leveraging, reaching out for what they need to turn their ideas into reality. Best of all, they're happy to share their stories authentically, chatting about successes and challenges so that others can also thrive.

Wikipedia is a great example of an ever-changing knowledge base that continues growing through the goodwill of people who share their knowledge with the world for free. Our first time meeting Uri Levine, cofounder of Waze, the amazing crowdsourced global positioning system (GPS) that Google bought for more than $1 billion, he said, "Ten years ago nobody heard of Wikipedia. Now, nobody's heard of Encyclopedia Britannica!" It's amazing how quickly the world turns. Platforms such as Facebook, Twitter, and LinkedIn allow us to share knowledge and experiences; open-source software, put together by incredibly smart people, provides us with amazing, free tools we can learn from and use.

At FreshBiz we always share our Action Cards and opportunities with our community freely and openly, and we encourage them to do the same for each other.

## It's Not All Fun and Games

Don't get us wrong; it's not all fun and games. The everyday lives of the New Entrepreneurz are not just about the tropical islands, fun collaborations, sexy tools, and free sources. They're also packed with challenges, lots of work, long nights, investments of savings, and financial uncertainty. Some days New Entrepreneurz have no clue what the next source of revenue might be. Some days they realize they might need to reinvent their entire business model from scratch. Other days they have to buckle down and write up an important document start to finish or mobilize an entire team, when what they'd prefer is just to sip a cold beer and watch a movie.

Challenges crop up all the time, which is why the New Entrepreneurz have a great sense of humor and love learning lessons. Sometimes businesses don't work out, sometimes students fail tests, sometimes the bottom drops out of a relationship, sometimes people get fired or the company closes down, and sometimes people lose their lifetime savings because of a financial breakdown. But this is life; it comes at a price, and the New Entrepreneurz take challenges in stride. They choose this lifestyle because at the end of the day, they know that with the right tools, skill set, and mind-set, they'll overcome all odds and live a life of purpose and self-expression.

Viewing themselves as Life Hackers and Gamers inherently lets New Entrepreneurz reduce some of the pressure that comes with playing the game called life. Too many people take life way too seriously, and when we say this we mean it with the full respect to the many life difficulties people face. This view is summed up excellently in the following quote from Mark Twain: "I am an old man and have known a great many troubles, but most of them never happened." Often, people are way more concerned with trying to solve problems that never happened than with continuing to roll the dice and move forward.

We see so many people stuck in a boring job just because they can't see past the problem of "What will happen if I can't find a new one?" instead of actually looking for a new one or even exploring the possibilities of starting their own businesses. We also meet people stuck in unsatisfying relationships or partnerships just because their imagination raises images of possible catastrophic outcomes, even though they realize their current status is far from paradise!

Entrepreneurial thinkers are always on the lookout for solutions, take into account potential outcomes, reduce risks by applying multidimensional thinking, know there'll be obstacles to overcome, and then go! Becoming an entrepreneurial thinker is just a question of what set of challenges you're willing to face.

Let's take a look at why some people aren't moving forward toward a better future. Often, our workshop participants describe their strong desire to change something in their lives—find a better job, start the business they've always dreamed about, change the quality of a personal relationship, or even move to a different city or country—but the bottom line is that they never take the necessary action.

Looking more deeply into why they don't take action, we find a recurring reason: fear of the price of change. But it's a fear that arises from an incorrect perception about what change costs. Considering switching to a new job, moving to a new city, or opening up to a new relationship, we tend to draw comparisons with what we might lose once we're out of the current situation. The thinking goes like this: "Of course I'd prefer a new job, one I really love, but what if I don't find it? I could end up losing the job I already have along with some of my savings." It might also go like this: "It'd be great to start my dream business, but what if I fail and lose my investment?"

This is a thought process that isn't going to serve your purposes. It's simple human nature that the fear of losing the familiar is always greater than the wish to step into a new unknown, making the comparison between loss and gain unfair.

Instead, we recommend you compare price versus price. Starting a business comes with a price. You might lose some money, go through a tough establishment period, need financing creativity, and have to work harder at the beginning, and yes, all that may mean you might have to spend less time with your family. These are prices you need to consider, if only to come up with ideas for potential solutions, but you also need to weigh the set of prices arising from *not* opening your dream business! Some of them include not realizing your true potential, having to live with lower self-esteem, understanding the negative message you send to your kids, having to comply with the demands of your tough and unforgiving boss, earning less than you think you could, and more. It's vital to understand that not taking action carries its own set of risks and prices.

We have a saying: "There's always a price to pay. The question is whether we're paying it to fulfill our dreams or maintain our fears."

What do *you* choose to pay for?

New Entrepreneurz choose to pay the price for fulfilling their dreams.

## Express Yourself

*To me, business isn't about wearing suits or pleasing stock-holders. It's about being true to yourself, your ideas and focusing on the essentials.*

—Richard Branson

What is entrepreneurship if not self-expression? Whether a new business, a social venture, or a family vacation, it's about you expressing yourself by creating a new reality from an idea.

As multidimensional creatures we realize there's no dichotomy between self-expression and making a living. Money and mission come together as a beautiful rainbow of products, services, and unique messages. As Henry Ford said many years ago, "A business that makes nothing but money is a poor business." This is truer now than ever before. Money is only one dimension. Values, on the other hand, are all encompassing.

Business is an extension of self-expression. Richard Branson is a prime example of the self-expressing entrepreneur. Through the vehicle of Virgin, he does business in music, airlines, banks, and space. Branson, Virgin, and his awesome team continuously amaze us with their adventures across many different industries that share a common denominator: the power of creative self-expression.

For New Entrepreneurz, starting a business is no longer just a form of making a living. *It is who they are.* Although we do need to make money and support our families, *just*

**Figure 2.3**   Joanna Braunold

making a living is the old-school approach. Nor do they look at a business as another type of job. Instead, business is a blank canvas waiting to be colored with their passions, values, and mission.

A company's successes used to be measured against a barometer of power, money, and its position on the Fortune 500. We used to believe that thousands of employees, acres upon acres of real estate, and billions of dollars in market value were the highest attributes of a successful business. For decades individuals and companies strived for these markers of success. Thank goodness that's changed! Today we have higher aspirations, and the New Entrepreneurz are the ones shining the beam of light on these new defining attributes of a great business.

If New Entrepreneurz consider the Fortune 500 an outdated model, what constitutes the new assessment model? Always believers of multiple streams of education, just like multiple streams of income, we at FreshBiz find ourselves constantly learning from educational programs. It was an inspiring TEDx Talk Andrew Hewitt, creator and founder of the GameChangers 500 (GC500), gave that really caught our attention. (Learn more about GC500 in the Interviews section at the back of the book.) In the talk, he explained how GC500 is the new game of business, awarding badges and achievements to purpose-driven companies that excel in different areas. It created badges to award companies for things such as innovation, ecofriendliness, work atmosphere, and global impact, among others. What's great is that none of the badges are connected with money, because on the

New Island, values are the drive for business, and money is simply a resource rather than the goal itself.

Having discovered GC500, a club we definitely felt was worth belonging to, we set ourselves a goal: to make it onto that list by 2014. Larger companies, such as Kickstarter, Google, and Zappos, along with smaller companies, such as 2 Degrees, Recology, Yes To, and Khan Academy, are all identified with this new type of purpose-driven business. We were so excited when GC500 chose to add FreshBiz to the list and award us our first few badges in the fields of innovation, meeting the mission, and everyone wins, to name a few. We also feel privileged to be the first company from the Middle East on the list and aspire to guiding other companies worldwide to achieve success through these values-based badges.

GC500 and some of the featured companies are excellent role models for concepts in this book. It was a pleasure interviewing them, and we will be presenting some of the best practices they shared with us. This will allow you as a reader to turn these concepts into everyday business life. Feel free to copy and paste because this is part of the new game of sharing, empowering, and inspiring.

### New Entrepreneurz Questions to Ponder

Here are two guiding questions you need to ask yourself as a New Entrepreneur.

*Question 1*: Is the initiative I am looking to launch (or the one I already have) a game worth playing?

In other words, do you really want to put the time, money, and energy into turning this idea into reality?

If the answer is yes:

*Question 2*: Why me?

In other words, why should you be the one doing it, doing this business, making this talk, or writing this book? What do you bring to the table that no one else can? How will this be a unique expression of your own voice?

Make sure you have genuine answers to these questions. You don't want to be making all that effort for the sake of just doing stuff or creating more me too, content that has already been done before. You deserve to be engaged in activities that are purpose driven and value driven, that let your soul sing and your unique voice be heard. The world loves freshness and is literally waiting for our new ideas and new systems. Separately and together, we have the resources to launch them all. Sing out loud and strong!

> *There's lots of bad reasons to start a company. But there's only one good, legitimate reason, and I think you know what it is: It's to change the world.*
>
> —Phil Libin, Evernote CEO

# 3 What Game Are You Playing?

*Do not train a child to learn by force or harshness; but direct them to it by what amuses their minds, so that you may be better able to discover with accuracy the peculiar bent of the genius of each.*

—Plato

**Figure 3.1**    Dalya Holder

## Life Is a Game

When we say life is a game, here's what we *don't* mean: That it's a joke, insignificant, or not challenging. What we *do* mean is that it's a journey limited only by time, with rules, skills, other players, and the goal to win. Winning is, of course, different for each person, but people normally desire to experience progress and fulfillment as they go through the stages of their lives, just like they would in a game. This is why game-based learning and gamification is gaining tremendous traction today, but we'll talk more about that later in the chapter.

At our game-based seminars, to help people zoom out from the board in front of them and carry the metaphor into their lives, we ask two main questions:

- What game are *you* playing?
- What does winning look like?

These aren't such simple questions to address, but addressing them is crucial because they essentially determine how you live your life.

So take all the time you need to think about those answers!

The time you invest in these questions is an opportunity to formulate and state for yourself the specific mission you seek to achieve. Describing your mission should not be influenced by the media or your parents and well-meaning family or friends, nor should it arise from jealousy aroused by looking at other people's successful games. It should come from your inner voice and the ideas that excite you specifically.

Look at your life as a movie. You, and no one else, are its star! But if you're not playing your own game, then you become one of the extras, a pawn in someone else's game. Here's another way of looking at it, famous from the world of poker: "If you can't spot the sucker at the table, then you are the sucker at the table." For too long the majority of people have unconsciously bought into other people's games, such as the game of economy and finance, education and training, health and nutrition, and more.

It's sad but true: The game many people are playing is one of competition. We've been programmed that way, so it's automatic at this point because our societies influence and train us to believe that it's the correct and healthy mode of living. We show up to school, summer camps, and colleges expecting competition; at our jobs the concept of promotion is an expectation of competition; and modern psychology's gotten us to expect competition with our partners in our business relationships, not to mention our personal relationships! It never stops. In truth, this competition is a complete figment of our imagination, a lie so prevalent that we experience it as real.

This book is designed to take you through a process of finding clarity on what some of the games the New Entrepreneurz play look like. Then see how they might fit you. After all, there's a price to pay for not creating new games and instead staying stuck in the collapsing, old ones. That price is now so high and pervades so many categories that it's unbearable for many of us. If the price of getting stuck is too high for you, then it's time to take action!

## The Old Games Are Broken, Outdated, and at Best Irrelevant

Across the spectrum, norms are cracking, a result of our playing the wrong games for too long. Let's just take a quick look at the global economy, as one example.

Let's start in the United States. At the time of this book's writing, 1 percent of Americans own around 40 percent of the wealth, whereas the lower-income 80 percent own around 7 percent, which isn't even enough for them to survive. According to recent statistics, at the start of 2014, some 20 million Americans are unemployed.

Per U.S. household, the average student loan debt is $32,000, and the average credit card debt is $15,000; this adds up to a total of more than $11 trillion of consumer debt. Just student loans alone in the United States broke $1 trillion, and that is debt that not even bankruptcy, as the city of Detroit and the country of Cyprus are looking into, can save you from.

Is this symptomatic of the United States alone? Let's turn the spotlight toward Europe. According to the summer 2013 census, unemployment rates for young adults under 25 in the European Union have become disturbing, bordering on frightening. France and Great Britain show around 25 percent unemployment, Italy logs in with 40 percent, and Greece and Spain are leading the way with close to 60 percent! How totally crazy that nearly 6 out of 10 young adults have no jobs or businesses, even though many of them invested thousands of dollars in a higher education degree that others told them would ensure a life of happily ever after!

Let's now take a direct trajectory, as the crow flies, from Europe to India. Currently, almost 700 million people will join the workforce within the next two decades. But there isn't enough work for everyone. Here's how to imagine 700 million: It's around the entire population of Europe inside the developing country of India!

Okay, so that's the economic and financial level, but what about physical health? In the United States, not only are more people dying from cancer, heart attacks, and stress than ever before but the obesity rate also went from 20 percent in 1997 to almost 40 percent in 2014 with almost 80 percent of the total population overweight. Here's one thought: Much of America's food produce is not approved for the European market's stringencies. Here's another thought: How can we even begin to calculate the total cost in decreased quality of life on people's financial, physiological, emotional, and spiritual levels?

In Chris Jordan's impactful TED Talk called "Turning Powerful Stats into Art," he cited the well-known statistic that 400,000 die from smoking cigarettes every year in the United States while 700,000 people under the age of 18 start smoking each year! That is unbelievable, especially when you look at it from this angle: Every other friend you have in the United States who starts smoking will die from it at some point.

How about this shocking fact: The fashion industry's impact together with media's onslaught on female self-esteem will influence some 350,000 American women to have elective breast surgery this year alone. It's apparently become so popular that over the past few years, breast surgery has become the number one graduation gift in America. Congratulations on your graduation! You may not have a job, or the ability to pay back your credit cards and loans, but at least you have shiny new boobs. All dressed up and nowhere to go!

One more shocking thing that Jordan shares is the sad environmental fact that in the United States, 4 million nonbiodegradable plastic cups and 40 million paper cups are thrown away *every day!* These paper cups alone translate into roughly 7 million trees a year being cut down so that people can enjoy their coffee to go.

It's not surprising that this is the end result of a process that starts from the moment we get into the educational system, described by Sir Ken Robinson as a glorified factory designed to strip us of our individuality, creativity, and divergent thinking. Latte, anyone?

If this sounds depressing, it's because it is. But it is only depressing right now because of all the bad seeds planted all those years, leading up to now. The good news is that the rat race is over, and the new era of entrepreneurial thinking is here. There is new hope and excitement as the New Entrepreneurz, who include solutionaries, game chang-ers, and influencers, plant new seeds and create fresh ways to play new games based on real values and real-value impact.

So let's explore some of the games that become possible when we get accustomed to thinking differently.

## The New Game of the Shared Economy, Multidimensional Thinking, and Ecofocus

Annie Leonard, creator of the videos "The Story of Stuff" and "The Story of Solutions," has made videos that demand we think and act smarter, by talking about playing the new game of *better* instead of *more*. Instead of pursuing more stuff backed up by more accessories for that stuff, Annie calls us to action to be better people creating better stuff that moves the world forward in the right direction. It would be nice if others thought like that, right?

Well, they do and they are starting to show and share it. We all know the famous Gandhi quote, "Be the change you want to see in the world."

We see this axiom finding its practical form in our workshops each time one person who's played the game of FreshBiz a few more times than the others transforms the table from competition into collaborative winning. It's beautiful in the context of a game. It's even better when we hear testimonials from FreshBizers who introduce this way of thinking into their industries and companies.

Think of all the new shared workspaces, hubs, and collaborative centers popping up around the globe where freelancers can work with each other as part of a community. They share space, resources, advice, and often clients as they work together to expand each other's activities. We predict that the next sitcoms on TV will be around the funny and fun-loving characters and lifestyles of the New Entrepreneurz at their shared workspaces. As Melissa Slim and Michelle

Woodward, two awesome female entrepreneurs, say, "Collaboration is the new competition."

More and more corporations are turning work into fun, as represented by the funky atmospheres at Google, Facebook, and Zappos, to name a few. The boardroom makes people bored. The new, cool spaces let people come together to share, generate feedback, and cocreate, rather than worry about putting the cover letter on their TPS report, like in the movie *Office Space*.

The new games that companies are playing are inspiring, empowering, and purpose-driven rather than hierarchical, ego-driven, and void of feelings. The new games are inspired by the new generation of Millennials. Our generation is asking questions and answering them by actively shaping the New Shared Economy we find ourselves in, a special place where access is more important than ownership.

"Access trumps ownership" are the three magic words we keep hearing. More people than ever find themselves asking new questions:

- Do I need to own the latest album by Newton Faulkner, Ninet, or the Pentatonix, or am I okay having access to their music through online radio and YouTube?

- Do I need to own all Seth Godin's or Michael Hyatt's books, or is being able to access some of them for free as Kindle library books enough for me?

- Must I own my home, or is having access to living indoors through renting, couch surfing, Airbnb, home exchange, or even house sitting more than okay for me?

- Is it important for me to own my own graphic designer or can having access to one through Fiverr and Elance serve my purposes just as adequately?

- Do I need to own a high school or college degree, or can access to knowledge through Coursera, Khan Academy, TED, and YouTube be all I need for my education?

- Must I own my car, or is a company lease, Uber, Sidecar, Lyft, or maybe even bicycle sharing something I can do fine with?

- Do I need to run out and buy all the recommended toys for every phase of my child's development, or can being part of a toy-sharing co-op achieve the same result?

. . . all for a fraction of the cost while being ecofriendly!

These are the real-life questions that typify the New Shared Economy as the old belief of "You are what you own" falls by the wayside. That belief is so 1980s Wall Street. The New Entrepreneurz believe that who you are equals the sum total of your experiences, skills, values, and tools wrapped in the right mind-set. Access to what you need when you need it means less hassle, more green, greater flexibility, and not locking into being overcommitted to paying for things you don't really need to own in the first place.

The best thing about the New Shared Economy isn't the access to stuff but rather the access to knowledge, people, and resources. Every time you look up something on Wikipedia or the Internet Movie Database (IMDb) or send a message to a connection on LinkedIn, you tap into the virtual shared economy. Also, let's not forget incredible avenues, such as crowdsourcing and crowdfunding via platforms such as Indiegogo, OurCrowd, and Kickstarter, which can help boost our greatest ideas into reality. Here's an awesome fact: Kickstarter proudly announced that as of 2014, it's raised a total of $1 billion from around the world to fund people's ideas. A billion dollars (gulp!) channeled to ideas that probably would have never seen the light of day if not for a great platform, an authentic video, worthwhile backer rewards, and an engaged community in the world of crowdfunding.

When we cut down substantially by choosing access over ownership and turn our small businesses into smart businesses, we can live leaner, freer, and healthier lives. It's also a lot more enjoyable and less stressful, too! Alexandra Liss is a great example of a New Entrepreneur synthesizing multidimensional thinking to create epic experiences. In a nutshell, she used Kickstarter to raise the money needed to couch surf her way through 80 countries over two years and then told her story in a compelling documentary called *One Couch at a Time*. Fun!

## The Battle of the Old Games Fighting the New Games

Where there is light, there are shadows. Where there is progress, there are forces that try to snuff out the progress. Many people built their fames, fortunes, and identities on the old world order. Obviously they aren't excited to see any familiar patterns change. They don't believe everyone can win the game. They're certain that winning necessitates losers. Seeing themselves as winning, they don't want change to jeopardize their status, so they want to keep things the way they are.

It's easy to spot old-school thinkers fighting against others reaching the New Shared Economy climate of the New Island. Back in 2000, the legendary Metallica and eventually much of the music industry went to battle to shut down Napster, the infamous open-source website that at its peak had 80 million users sharing MP3s of their favorite music. They chose to go out to battle instead of adapting to the new game of music by innovating and creating a new business model that aligned with the new technology. Ultimately, Steve Jobs and Apple did it with iTunes.

Recently, because of the scarcity and therefore inflated value of taxi medallions needed to be registered cab drivers, taxi cartels in cities such as Chicago and San Francisco were ganging up and working hard to shut down affordable ride-sharing platforms, such as Uber. Lyft, Uber, and similar platforms allow people access to great car service driven by local people who are accessible by smartphone and provide their services for less than the cost of a typical taxi fare. This is again a great example of an old industry choosing to invest its energy in fighting new technologies instead of choosing to reinvent itself.

How about New York City trying to block Airbnb from operating within its city? What could be the problem with an awesome service that allows residents around the world to make some extra money by renting out their own homes or rooms for reasonable prices, you ask? Well, apparently the hotels and other connected institutions don't appreciate the competition. They're fighting hard to label Airbnb as a platform for illegal hotel operators who avoid taxes and even threaten safety. Thank you, New York City, for being so concerned about our safety, but we'd prefer to have affordable and interesting options that are more in the spirit of Win to the Winth Power for the people.

But meanwhile it's somehow okay for governments to bail out morally bankrupt banks, financial institutions, and other companies that are, so they say, too big to fail, so that the old-game controlling parties' powers can be kept intact.

Here is something interesting that we came across online: New technologies have been developed that can lower electricity costs by 93 percent. But old-game governments and huge powerful for-profit corporations have been intervening, blocking, and sabotaging this information from getting out to the entrepreneurs and engineers who could take this public. Notice something? Government promotes ecofriendly yet continues to support old-game players whereas the truly ecofriendly new-game players are derided. We have yet to figure that one out.

> *Earth provides enough to satisfy every man's need, but not every man's greed.*
>
> —Gandhi

## Closing Questions to Ponder

- Do you find yourself playing the wrong game with people when you could be playing the right one?

- Do you like the role you are playing in business and relationships?

- Do people feel good when they engage in a relationship with you?

- How can you change the rules of what you're doing to be more in line with the new?

There are countless more examples of people with old-school mind-sets looking to block the new light from shining upon us. We might still have some way to go, but as we see it, it's up to us to keep moving, aspiring, and elevating. The deeper we examine and unravel the games we play in life and their old-game limitations, the more we can shift or create new game avenues that inspire Win to the Winth Power.

## Gamifying Your Life

*We do not stop playing because we get old; we get old because we stop playing.*

—Benjamin Franklin

The New Shared Economy is the New Entrepreneurz' favorite playground. We'll provide more description of how it looks in the next chapter. For now, let's show you what it looks like when we gamify life!

### Throw the Dice

There are two outcomes of throwing the dice. If it's a luck game, such as craps, throwing the dice represents a gamble: You either win or lose. But if it's a game of skills, such as CashFlow, FreshBiz, or the game of real life and business,

**Figure 3.2**   Dayla Holder

then throwing the dice is how you take action and make things happen.

For us, the important one is the second one, where throwing the dice is how you move forward. We could say that on a metaphysical level, throwing the dice is how we collaborate with the universe. In other words, when we make a move, it makes a move back, linking us. If we move in the right direction, positive feedback is returned. If we move in a direction that's not good for us, we're rewarded with an important lesson to learn.

Here's an example of what we mean: In January 2012, one of our facilitators from France excitedly told Ronen about his upcoming plans to fly to the United States and attend the Unleash the Power Within weekend seminar run by Tony Robbins. Because this seminar was one of the experiences on Ronen's bucket list, he decided to throw the dice and bought a ticket as well. Now that Ronen was going to be going to the United States anyway, he presented Simcha with the idea of reaching out to his best U.S. contacts and setting up some high-level workshops for the week before the big seminar. Simcha threw the dice, connected with his best people in Texas, and set up a workshop there that had to be canceled one day before it was scheduled to take place because their flight from New York to Texas was canceled.

"For the first few minutes we were totally bummed," Simcha relates. "After all, the people who made the workshop arrangements really went out on a limb for us, and there wasn't going to be an opportunity to reschedule it for that trip. Ronen and I felt bad disappointing them. As compensation, the airline offered us free flights anywhere else in the United States. Initially we jumped for joy and started high-fiving each other. We could go climb the Rockies in Colorado, play poker in Vegas, catch sunshine in Miami . . . but one look out the window led us to a different choice. We hadn't lost anything; actually, we'd just gained three extra days in New York, one of the coolest cities in the world, and that decision later led to unlocking amazing connections at Pace University, which we mentioned earlier."

For now, let's get back to the story. In the end, Ronen left a week later for the Tony Robbins seminar with more than 5,000 participants in New Jersey. On its first day, Tony picked Maria out of the massive crowd of people, calling her onstage to share one of her life challenges. Maria spoke about how she loves being an entrepreneur and wants to coach others toward great out-of-the-box lives but was constricted by her parents' old-fashioned belief systems. Hearing her speak, Ronen felt compelled to meet her because what she'd shared completely jibed with the FreshBiz methodology and mission. It's always challenging to find a needle in a haystack, but when your haystack is about 5,000 people, on a day that starts at 11 AM but doesn't end until deep into the night at around 2 AM, with walking on fire and barely any breaks, finding Maria was close to a mission impossible.

On the second day after an exercise in which Ronen jotted down some of his limiting beliefs about himself, including how he sometimes feels trapped by his shyness, the participants were finally let out for their first break. Suddenly, with just 5 minutes of the break remaining, a miracle occurred:

He spotted Maria! But she was surrounded by a group of enthusiastic fans who, to Ronen, seemed like an insurmountable wall. He faced the choice: conquer his shyness during the next seminar exercise or conquer it in real life right now. Ronen rolled the dice and went all-in! Walking confidently over to Maria, he introduced himself.

"Hi, my name's Ronen. I'm from Israel. I came to the United States for this seminar, and because of a brand-new entrepreneurial game and workshop I created called FreshBiz."

Maria looked at him, stunned and speechless, until she said, "I was one of the people waiting for you at the Texas workshop! I was so upset when it got canceled!"

My, how the universe creates miracles and gives feedback for those who just keep on rolling the dice!

## It Is Never "Just" a Game

*Education is teaching our children to desire the right things.*

—Plato

Games are food for the mind. They are fun and engaging and therefore powerful, so please play the right ones.

From Monopoly to the Game of Life, society's been teaching kids the wrong lessons about money, success, competition, ambitions, and values. Think about the huge success of Grand Theft Auto, where, if the screen is large enough, you can literally experience yourself beating old ladies, hijacking people's cars, dealing drugs, and killing police officers who annoyingly try to stop you!

It's a huge mistake to think that a game is only a game. We now know that's not true. Games are not just a break in reality: They mold our reality. Games shape our outlook, opinions, and conclusions. Games guide what and how we learn. This is how it's always been, and how it always will be. We start playing games as kids, then continue into adult life playing adjusted games that rely on the skills and values we collected along the way.

Yet even though we find ourselves in a new world, we continue playing old games that reinforce the wrong values. Change the games you, your kids, and your community are playing, and you'll essentially change your game of life. That's where the difference lies. That's where our personal mission in the world lies as well!

## The Power of Games

Studies show that about 90 percent of our habits are automatic. We're wired that way and for the most part, it serves us well. We don't need to relearn how to drive each time we get into a car, nor do we need to rethink what to do every time the traffic light turns green. Muscle memory allows us to get back on a bicycle and find balance, to pick up a guitar and strike an E chord, and to get Grandma's lemon cake recipe right while holding the baby and mentally running through tomorrow's presentation even when we are exhausted.

The problem arises when we find ourselves automatically responding to situations in ways that do not serve our best interests, such as getting angry, placing blame on others, or becoming paralyzed with fear. Most often, these manifestations occur because of the pattern of past experiences and responses that we hardwired into the software that runs our brains.

If you've ever participated in a self-development workshop or worked with a business coach, then you already know that bringing new quality into your life means it's imperative to change the way you think and act. This process basically calls for a rewiring of the brain. Its net of neurological connections fires electric charges that instruct the body how to act. It's a highly effective machine, and therefore the more we do a particular sequence of actions, the stronger the brain connections grow between the relevant neurons.

To change the way we act, we need to break down old connections and build new ones. Here is how games come into the picture as an incredible platform for this type of development. Rewiring our brains means training them to continue thinking and acting differently long enough for the new connections to be forged. Instead of working out our muscles in the gym, we can work our mental muscles in the fitness center of our mind to create muscle memory.

There are two ways to achieve rewiring.

The first way is to go out there and begin doing things in a new and different way. For many people, leaving their comfort zone is a scary process and therefore is *un*comfortable. The greater the distance from the comfort zone, the greater the discomfort, and the easier it is to give up. Just think of the last time you promised yourself that you'd wake up at 5 AM for an early fresh-air run or that the delicious chocolate donut at the office meeting is really worth skipping. Maybe you even kept your promise—for a few days, but then somehow you found yourself back in the old habits. We've all been there! That's because in all these cases, the brain never had the right conditions for rewiring.

The second way to retrain your brain is by playing games—the right ones. It's highly effective because it's lasting, and that's because of an amazing fact: Brains don't care whether any specific moment's experience is real or not. The brain simply creates a relevant activity that elicits a physical response in your body. Case in point: Imagine yourself back in the classroom with one wall covered by a massive chalkboard. The teacher accidentally causes the chalk to scrape across the board or, maybe even worse, runs her nail over it. Did you just experience a full-body shiver and some goose bumps like we just did? Cool, right? You experienced a bodily reaction merely by raising an old memory into your brain. No real board, no chalk, no nail, and no teacher. Just you and your brain.

Playing games allows us to trick the brain by leveraging this idea to develop new skills and implement new behaviors, which rewire our brains, all within the safety of a game. Because games are fun, they're easier to stick with than consciously fighting old habits. The more you play, the stronger the leveraged connections become. That's why you should always play the right games!

In the FreshBiz game, players repeatedly experience higher levels of skills in negotiation, collaboration, spotting opportunities, and creative thinking, to name just a few of the areas in which our brains are activated. These abilities are improved and refined with each game played. It's mind-blowing to see the direct correlation between the number of times people play the game and improvement to their real life skills and mind-set, which help create real life success.

Here's a great story: We were amused to learn that a group of Nobel Prize–winning Spanish neuroscientists gave up on a test they wanted to run with FreshBiz players because the FreshBiz game is so multidimensional that it simultaneously activates more areas of the brain than they'd be able to measure. The neuroscientists simply lacked the technology to map all the simultaneous brain activity occurring during game play!

## Let's Play the "Get to the Island Game"!

Here's a new game avenue to inspire Win to the Winth Power and muscle memory in *you*.

The definition of entrepreneurial thinking is turning ideas into reality, and we love nothing better than putting things into action. Because *actually* experiencing the game is the best way we've found to put ideas into action, we've designed a special game for you. Remember, this book is to open your mind to actually change the way you play life, not just read about it or think about it. The goal is: Read, reread, and implement immediately.

Getting to the New Island is the goal of the FreshBiz game, both on the board itself and on the board of your life. This is the metaphor describing the new mind-set needed for a purpose-driven, value-driven life.

But seriously, wouldn't it be cool to actually meet on the New Island? Play, learn, connect, and have some fun, all on a real island? We think so, too, and that's why we designed something special for you!

As a reader of *The New Entrepreneurz,* twice a year you'll have an opportunity to join us on a real island, somewhere in the world, for a few days of experiences, workshops, networking, and fun with other like-minded entrepreneurial thinkers across all spectrums of life.

What does it take to get there? The will, time, and money, which can all be generated with the right tools, skills, and mind-set! If you have the will, then we have the way. As you go through the chapters of the book, we'll throw in some tips and tricks on how to play life so that you can generate the time and money needed to celebrate on the New Island with us.

So let's get you building some gamified brain muscle memory around getting to the New Island—not as a concept, but as your new reality!

Get started by going to the New Island game website at www.thenewislandgame.com. There, you'll be able to track your progress, meet and collaborate with other players, collect tips and tricks, share Action Cards, and play your way to the New Island.

Play until you make it, and we'll celebrate together.

See you on the other side!

# 4 Win to the Winth Power

*A mind, once expanded by a new idea, never returns to its original dimensions.*

—Oliver Wendell Holmes

**Figure 4.1**  Kinamon Ron

C rossing over to the New Island will have you saying good-bye to the old mind-sets and moving forward to embrace the new.

## The Three Zip Codes and the Island

Imagine you've chosen to set out on your adventure; you're in the car, buckled up, and ready to go. Excitedly you pull out of the driveway onto the main road. You're finally leaving the noisy, polluted, chaotic city of LoseDeLosa. On the radio, Annie Lennox is singing her song about sweet dreams for those who want to abuse and be abused, and you think, *Wow, what a coincidence!* The words totally describe the destructive policies governing LoseDeLosa, where everyone plays life and business as though they're in a dog-eat-dog world. Just the other day your acquaintance, on the way to ripping off a few people at work, told you about this online computer game she's been playing called LoseLose, where each time she kills another player's alien, her opponent loses an actual computer file, and each time she blasts one of the spaceships into smithereens, her opponent loses an actual application. You can't help thinking that mutually abusive relationships never really should have had a place in human history, but they've definitely outstayed their time. Over shouts and crowds of violence, you manage to drive out.

Through the car's open window comes a cool breeze from the approaching village of WinLosso. That already gets you feeling better. WinLosso's got a better energy to it. You can sense the excitement of winning and think about how much fun it can be to celebrate strength and victory. There's only one problem in this village. Every win comes with a price: a loss. Every victory one person achieves breaks someone else. That pervades the village with a bittersweet atmosphere of zero-sum competition, where a person needs to work harder than everyone else, outsmart the competition, sabotage opponents, and decimate others they define as enemies, no matter what expense is involved, just so they can *win!* At least here, winning is possible.

It doesn't matter at all if the opponents are left with no job; no way to care for their marriages, families, or health; and no self-esteem. Then the winner comes along and becomes a big philanthropist, doling out large sums of money to support culture or to support less privileged people. You wonder: *Surely some of those anonymous people and their families now being supported by the big winner's funds were once the big winner's competition—wouldn't it have been better just to bypass that stage?* Looking at the full picture of what winning looks like here in the village of WinLosso is quite sobering, now that you think about it.

That's why you'll keep your foot on the gas pedal and continue driving through to the next place, the town of WinWinna. Perched on the peak of an impressive mountain overlooking the sea, the town is thriving! Every winner has a match somewhere else; shops offer products that are simultaneously helpful, smart, and pleasant; the educational system opens access to resources that make it possible for WinWinna's residents to accomplish their visions and be fulfilled; and relationships beautifully weave micro and macro together. The atmosphere here not only feels healthier, but families also literally look more wholesome. What could be better than all parties winning?

WinWinna's breathtaking, you decide. You're just about to get out of your car and celebrate your arrival, but you look across the water at the New Island of Win to the Winth Power. It appears as majestic and epic as Oz must have appeared to Dorothy. Knowing deep down that that's your real destination, you find yourself already back in the car for the last leg of the drive to the island. Crossing over is what's next for you. Crossing over is what you've set your sights on, especially because you know how valuable it will be to you and everyone else in your life to choose the most expanded mind-set.

Win to the Winth Power, here we come!

The key to enter the island of the New Entrepreneurz is letting go of lose-lose, win-lose, and even sometimes win-win to achieve the extraordinary: Win to the Winth Power, the place where multidimensional winning goes above and beyond in quality and quantity. It's no longer just two of us winning but also our parents and families, other people we're in touch with, and even the countries of all those people. In other words, everyone's winning in numerous and varied simultaneous dimensions.

It's fast to drive seamlessly through zip codes, right?

Getting to the new mind-set of Win-to-the-Winth-Power thinking can happen faster than you'd think possible. In the game of FreshBiz, it can actually take less than 90 minutes.

## The New Mind-Set

Win to the Winth Power is your ticket to generating expansive results. Keep asking the question, "Who can I help win her or his game while I go about doing what I'm doing anyhow?" and then follow that question with "And who else?" Instead of killing two birds with one stone and finding you've got two dead birds, neither of which will ever produce eggs again, how can you win 2, 5, or 10 games simultaneously with one action?

This is how Yosef Adest, the Tel Aviv mastermind behind 52Frames, created his exceptional project for artists around the world. (Learn more about Yosef in the Interviews section at the back of the book.) Here's how the game works: Each and every week of the year, the community of photographers otherwise known as Framers go out with their cameras to capture and then share the theme of that week. The results are breathtaking photos and an incredible multidimensional win! Just think about it; Yosef lives his dream of being an artist surrounded by artists, and his community of photographers and wannabe photographers get to express their artistic voice on a weekly basis, while getting to grow, learn, and develop, all while their families and friends get to enjoy an artistically rich experience of seeing fresh photos each week. Then, of course, we got to win also. We selected our favorite images that best represent each chapter of the book to celebrate this project that has opened up so many doors to artists from all over!

This is how to play the game for the greatest fun factor possible because it creates huge momentum, great collaborations, and expanded leverage! This is how the New Entrepreneurz achieve the incredible things they do, and this is how you will, too.

Practice, practice, practice!

There's a great story Simcha loves to tell because it demonstrates how he turned walking his son each morning into multiple wins in different dimensions of life, which we call Win to the Winth Power. Always keen on multidimensional winning and family time, Simcha takes his son for a walk each morning in the stroller. Not only is walking his baby boy for an hour each day a great way to start the day, establishing special quality time with each other, but it also makes for great exercise. Of course, in addition to having an hour-long fitness routine in the morning, it allows time for thinking, singing, and a healthy dose of sunshine and vitamin D. It's an activity that guarantees he gets out of the house at least once a day to enjoy healthy quality time.

Because Simcha also enjoys thinking about how to take things further, he posed himself a question: Could he somehow create income while enjoying the walk? The question didn't arise because he felt he must create an additional financial resource, because life isn't about monetizing everything, but simply for the fun of the game. He asked his wife, Rachel, a successful real estate agent in Jerusalem, for postcards that advertise her services, explaining that he'd drop them in mailboxes along a different street each day. She printed thousands of them. Seven months into this morning ritual, they calculated that Rachel closes one extra deal every other month from these efforts! Based on conservative statistics, Simcha estimates an extra few thousand dollars per month comes into the family pot and therefore an extra few hundred dollars a month that they get to give to charity. Not bad for spending quality time with his son, which he was going to do anyway!

Through this sweet story we can see how through one simple activity, you can create wins in many aspects of your life. From getting some exercise and sunshine, to spending quality time with the kids, to gaining some extra income, this is what Win to the Winth Power looks like! Feel free to copy and paste the activities above or the mind-set.

If, one day, others look at your life, and see what appears to be magic and miracles happening, you'll be able to tell them confidently: Try Win-to-the-Winth-Power thinking!

# 5  Action Cards

*Do you want to know who you are? Don't ask. Act! Action will delineate and define you.*

—Thomas Jefferson

**Figure 5.1**    Sara Raanan

## What Are Action Cards?

Action Cards are the avenues that allow you to quantify the gifts, talents, skills, connections, and knowledge that you usually don't count as assets or options. Action Cards let all of us experience the value and power of everything we have going for us that until now was probably invisible to us. Action Cards are the currency that lets us unlock opportunities and experiences, move us forward in life, and achieve our greatest goals. Your car, an amazing online group you belong to, your savvy cooking skills, a knack for Spanish or remembering names, or your friend in London—they're all Action Cards you can use and share creatively.

In the game of FreshBiz itself, all players start with five Action Cards, which they can use whenever and wherever they like. Each one is completely unique, and more can be picked up along the way. It's up to us to figure out the smartest times to play an Action Card so that it provides us with its best value. Also, as in life, players don't have to wait to use them. They don't need to wait for someone's turn, someone's approval, or even the seemingly perfect moment. They just need to recognize the cards and activate them.

Action Cards are literally everywhere waiting for you to identify and use them, so go do so, and apply Win-to-the-Winth-Power thinking to enjoy playing with a whole new currency at a whole new level!

Ask people to name three well-known currencies. What are the chances they'll say dollars, euros, British pounds, or maybe even Bitcoins? What are the chances they'll go for currencies that are *completely other* than money—such as Action Cards?

Well, the better we get at leveraging them, the better our lives get as well.

How frequently do you hear of friends or family who say they feel stuck because they lack money? But allowing an insufficiency in just one form of currency to determine how stuck one is demonstrates a very one-dimensional perspective. Viewing money as the only currency that can promote forward movement or manifest dreams and wishes causes people to view themselves as having almost no options. The conclusion: They feel limited or incompetent.

A simple shift, a zoom out and away from the strangle-hold of money on their thinking, and they can see the wealth of their entire collection of Action Cards, see how to access them, and see the endless multidimensional opportunities they provide. For us at FreshBiz, we have traveled many countries, reached amazing people, and formed long-lasting relationships through the power of leveraging Action Cards. This chapter aims to help you unlock the power of currencies available to you that have been concealed from your sight until now.

## Myriad Forms of Currency

Currency was created as a way to measure and pay for trad-able goods and services. Two of the most ancient currencies were salt and carob seeds, which are said to have an identical weight and gave rise to the word *carat,* now used to measure gold and precious gems. It wasn't long before the term *currency* became synonymous with *money*. At some point, humans began putting currency up on a pedestal and began worshiping it, battling and warring over it, seizing others' land because of it, and creating comparative scales of value for goods and services, instead of enjoying the experiences that currency opened up. But as multidimensional creatures, our currency systems need to be multidimensional, too. We call these multidimensional systems or currencies *Action Cards* and relegate money to being just one dimension in a never-ending array of Action Cards. So let's get really good at using, playing, and sharing them! Keep in mind that they aren't for collecting, hoarding, or using later, like money and diplomas. Action Cards are made for playing.

We've met workshop participants who are convinced that because they're poor, their life can be nothing but pain and frustration when in actuality, they could be holding a royal treasury of Action Cards they've never thought about or just don't see. What can that feeling be likened to? Walking around in a room so dark that you feel blind, and forgetting there's a full box of matches in your pocket. Light one, and the whole room's illuminated.

## What Action Cards Can Do

This chapter was written in New York. Here is how we leveraged our Action Cards instead of money to create an unforgettable experience.

We flew to the United States and spent two nights in an incredible New York City hotel once we got there without using any money. Thank you, credit cards, miles, and points!

We were given a cell phone, a car, and a beautiful lakeside cabin for five nights in upstate New York where we could write the book, without using any money. Thank you, amazing family!

We met with some of New York's top boutique public relations companies and influencers, without using any money. Thank you, LinkedIn Pro account!

All in all, it was an incredible adventure that came together through a handful of Action Cards, great relationships, and the ability to weave them together nicely, which we call multidimensional thinking. There we were, writing at Swan Lake with deer eating from the apple trees right outside our door and the fall foliage covering the ground in electric oranges, yellows, greens, and reds. Thank you, Action Cards, for this great experience!

Action Cards are awesome when . . .

1. You've clearly identified yours.

2. You've clearly identified those of others.

3. You have a keen sense of their different values, depending on who's using them.

4. You choose great moments to use them.

5. You show them, share them, play them, sell them, trade them, and give them away.

The New Entrepreneurz combine Action Cards as skillfully as ancient weavers of intricate tapestries, and they reinforce everything else while doing so. Many of our FreshBizers who have been through some of the higher-level seminars share about how they palpably experience the richness, opportunities, and fun in their life through playing Action Cards wherever they go—they make for amazing stories!

We love the feedback that we receive from around the world when participants complete their first workshop, called Win to the Winth Power. We hear people talking about how they never realized how many real-life Action Cards they have to play or how great their Action Card wealth really is. There is also a huge shift in achievable possibilities through Action Cards when you view the people around you as teammates rather than competitors.

## For All You Professionals out There

LinkedIn is an Action Card generator for literally endless connections and opportunities. One click and you have instantaneous access to top influencers, GameChanger 500 companies, great groups, and extraordinary people. Want to win the game of LinkedIn? Know who you are and who you are looking for. Here's a simple tip: Having the basic LinkedIn account gives you the ability to join up to 50 groups. Did you know that? You can tap into 50 different worlds of the type of people you want to hear, share with, hang out with, and experience life with—that's gazillions of Action Cards just in this one area of LinkedIn that can transform your professional life at whatever level you are on. And it's free! So never ever be a part of less than 50 groups. Why would you? You gain 50 streams of information, education, and transformation by knowing what you want to join. Some of our best FreshBiz partners around the globe came through getting linked in online and then transforming that relationship offline.

## Priceless versus Worthless

Don't undervalue an Action Card because it doesn't have a specific monetary value. Want to know what else doesn't have value? The necklace that used to belong to your great-grandmother and the clock that once belonged to your uncle's uncle, but we call them priceless, not worthless, and we cherish them.

You are an influencer if you care more about affecting a few million people than making a few million dollars. This is the origin of the *pay with a tweet* concept. In other words, we would prefer that your entire tribe of Twitter followers hear from you about our product or service than you purchase it from us for a few bucks. New Entrepreneurz find and create value by playing their Action Cards with the people who value those cards most.

Phillip McKenzie and Jon Levy are two amazing people we are blessed to know, who run two types of platforms for influencers. They truly understand the power of influencers and their wide array of Action Cards. When Phillip McKenzie approached us to speak on the stage of the first Influencer Conference in Israel, we were really impressed by the concept and by him as well. (Learn more about Phillip and Jon in the Interviews section at the back of the book.) Realizing the power of the influencer culture to shape the future across different industries and disciplines, he created the platform known as InfluencerCon to give these amazing leaders the arena to share their ideas, innovations, and thoughts. Basically, this event is an Action Cards party that has nothing to do with business or money necessarily; people just get together and see how they can bring value to each other in any way possible. This is what we call the Action Card economy, and we invite you to look for or create opportunities like these in your communities.

Whereas Phillip creates influencer events for the public, our friend Jon Levy crafted a more intimate event that he calls Influencers Dinner. Jon is a playful entrepreneur who puts on these monthly dinners in his Upper West Side apartment with incredible influencers because he realized that living a powerful life involves two things: quality people and quality conversations. The idea behind the event is simple; he gathers 10 people to a Friday night dinner, where they get to cook together and engage in quality conversations. It's an invitation-based event, where none of the guests know who the other guests will be before they arrive, and to keep things pure, they can't talk about who they are or what they do for the first hour while preparing dinner together. To get this exclusive invitation, you have to meet only one term: Be rich in Action Cards.

Since he started this a few years ago, he has already been featured in the *New York Times* and *Forbes* magazine and has had guests who are movie stars, musicians, Olympic medalists, comic book sensations, and incredible business entrepreneurs as well. After having a few hundred guests over for dinner, Jon has now leveraged this by opening an influencer company that matches the right people with the right products and services.

It's time to get good at distinguishing your Action Cards and those of others!

## Action Cards—I'll Show You Mine, If You Show Me Yours

Start viewing the world as a big community where you can showcase and share your gifts, talents, and strengths, without fear or vulnerability. Join and create communities of people who share this mind-set, and play those Action Cards as a form of self-expression! We call it an Action Card co-op. Here's an idea to ponder. What might happen to homework and exams if, in every classroom, all the children's Action Cards were posted on a list, making them available for all other pupils—or even mentoring staff—to use? Same idea for start-ups or corporations: Imagine if everyone's names and Action Cards were clearly displayed on a wall in every meeting area or workstation to promote collective winning. Let's make this close up and personal now: What if each family had an Action Card list in a designated place? Parents and siblings could ascertain how each family member can contribute, play a role, and move the family forward. Plant an Action Card garden in your community, and just watch what amazing things happen. People naturally want to share, want to influence, and want to do what they are good at. This is the perfect platform that lets everyone expand what each other is doing!

When you start opening your Action Cards for other people, you'll start to notice how many people will begin to open up and share their Action Cards with you, too. This is much like that basic lesson in sales: Smile at someone and she or he will smile, too; nod to that person and she or he will inevitably wind up nodding back. Reaching out to others creates a flow of abundance and a fluidity that feels warm, nice, and wholesome. This doesn't operate on tit for tat. Instead, it's just an open space for connecting and empowering. The top-level executive at Sony Music might just be your mom's brother, whom you call Uncle Harry, but he could also be the dream come true for your friend and her band. Make the connection and let them know that you are open to sharing Action Cards. Then invite others to play life with that mentality as well. Remember: These are Action Cards, not power cards. The connections aren't about your ego, your pride, or your taking advantage of people. It's about creating action that moves the world forward. It's about winning the game of value-based living through helping yourself and others simultaneously win or at least get really far ahead.

It used to be that people kept their Action Cards close to their chest, turning them into power cards. In the world of the New Entrepreneurz, concealing your Action Cards is selfish and detracts from you as a person and from what's possible for the world as a whole. When you hide your Action Cards, you're essentially communicating that you do not trust people and that you yourself cannot be trusted because you understand why they are hiding their Action Cards from you as well.

Learn to leverage your Action Cards, and watch how quickly you expand experiences!

Here are some more fun Action Card wins:

- Ronen's wife, Anat, is a talented graphic designer who designed the first FreshBiz game.
- Simcha's power-packed smoothie-making skills scored him a great weeklong couch surf in Amsterdam.
- Our amazing partner Josh translated the game from Hebrew into English and connected with the right people online, which unlocked our global activities.
- Yosef and Or, our friends and FreshBizers, are talented photographers and videographers whom we work with on our projects and send customers to in need of quality work.

The list goes on and on.

## Now That You've Identified Your Action Cards, What Happens Next?

Two simple steps:

1. Start by writing down five Action Cards today.
2. Begin sharing them with people in your life.

Keep in mind that you benefit from Action Cards when you *use* them. They're not artwork to be collected and displayed. Action Cards have no value if you don't put them into *action*. So don't hide them in a vault or selfishly protect them for later. Use them now. Activate them! Imagine if the divine hand Michelangelo painted, reached down every month and snatched away 10 of your real-life Action Cards! You'd be a lot more motivated to wake up each morning with a carpe diem attitude toward them. Sure, it might not be the optimal time for you to play them, but it's still better than not having them to play at all.

Keep in mind the famous quote, "Perfect is the enemy of the good."

## Eight Reasons Why People *Don't* Share Action Cards

If Action Cards are so valuable, potentially even more so than money, why would people not share them? Here are the eight reasons that we have found:

1. They don't know what Action Cards are.

2. They don't know what Action Cards they specifically have.

3. They undervalue their own Action Cards.

4. They have been trained not to share or even show their hand.

5. Talking about Action Cards seems like bragging or showing off.

6. They were raised with a competitive mind-set, which is the false notion that sharing with another will let the other win first or instead of.

7. They have an ego and want the credit because it's *their* Action Cards.

8. They fear that the person gaining from the Action Cards may use it against them or may not need them anymore.

## Use Them at Work

Many people don't share Action Cards because they don't understand their language. Here is a simple idea on how you can make a difference in the culture of your business or corporation, just by picking a day and time. For example, call it Action Card Wednesday! Every Wednesday from noon to 1 PM at work, you and your coworkers will begin freely sharing Action Cards.

Tom is first on the list. He's from marketing but someone in his family owns the local theater, so he's hooking up coworkers with free movie tickets. Wendy from accounting is sharing her two library cards so that coworkers can download free e-books that automatically are returned after a couple of weeks. A free hour of tutoring is being given by Michael from human resources. He's demonstrating how to take great pictures with an iPhone and explaining the cool, free apps that turn photos into winners. Last, Maria is giving Spanish lessons to those who would like them, and she would love to learn from whoever can teach her about grants and scholarships that her son could apply for as he continues his education. How great would this be? As more and more people learn about the culture of Action Cards, they start to transform their local cultures, and it is making all the difference!

## Use Them at College

What would life look like if a group of students created Action Card Thursdays before going out to party for the weekend? Melissa, who's a biology whiz, shares her notes with everyone and even helps those who have trouble with a particular unit in that week's studies. Carlos, who has his own key to the student union, invites everyone in for 2 hours of TED Talks weekly to recharge thinking. Jason has got the credit card game down pat and shows everyone how to access free spring and winter break vacations. Rachel, who knows how to use LinkedIn efficiently, mentors her peers on how to set themselves up with the best people and companies for work around school and work upon graduation.

Here's a real-life example: Tony Hsieh, who runs Zappos and wrote the amazing book *Delivering Happiness,* shares a great story on how he needed 20 questions answered for a test back at his university. He asked 20 of his bright classmates simply to answer one question each and then offered to share all the answers with them! That's collaborative winning through smarts and Action Cards.

## Share Action Cards

We say *share* and not *barter* because when people want to barter, they often mean tit for tat. I'll do this one specific thing if you do this one specific thing. That requires deciding on the precise values and making sure that things are completely fair and equal. When we share Action Cards, we just share them, understanding that as multidimensional people living multidimensional realities, sometimes you'll get more value and sometimes the other person will get more value. Instead of weighing and measuring pennies based on the Old Island system, a goodwill-sharing attitude creates a flow, a team, and winning. It says, "I care less about the details of who got more in this one specific case and more about both of us winning overall." Small minds that focus on the specifics of tit for tat are playing a game of jealousy and unfairness whereas people playing Action Cards are simply having a blast expanding life for each other.

## Know the Value of Action Cards

Action Cards have different values, depending on who uses them. As we mentioned earlier, in the game of FreshBiz, you can play an Action Card called "collect profits." If you play a selfish game and focus only on yourself, then the maximum value based on the businesses you've bought throughout the game might bring in $1 million. On the other hand, zoom out for a moment, and look at the resources and businesses of other players. What you're doing is looking at how you can bring value to the team, and now you see a different picture altogether. You might be sitting across from Jennifer, who has $3 million in potential business profits. Hmm, how can that be used to leverage greater potential? You go for straight communication, wanting to get both of you to a winning spot.

"Hey, Jennifer, want to make a million dollars in less than 5 seconds?" you ask.

"Uh, sure!" she answers.

"Take my Action Card, collect your profits of 3 million, give me 2 million so that I can double what I would have collected by myself, and take 1 million for yourself as a thank-you for making the deal happen."

"Okay, cool!"

Here are some of the outcomes that might have occurred instead, and often do when people first play the game. Jennifer might be used to the world of sales and negotiations and might instinctively try to negotiate a 50/50 split because often that's how salespeople are trained. They're not used to someone making such a good deal with them on the first try. Well, I can either give in and we each make $1.5 million or explain to her that making $1 million more than what she has right now because of my creativity and Action Card is actually providing her with a lot more than she had in the first place. Letting greed cloud our vision bogs us both down. Jennifer, raised on Old Island systems, also might be convinced that life's a competition and therefore doesn't want me to get ahead because that translates in her mind into thinking she's somehow being beaten. It sounds absurd but I've played the game of FreshBiz with people who think the only way to run faster than other people is by breaking the others' legs. It takes some training and practice to play collaboration and communicate straight through the prism of Win to the Winth Power. But playing this type of game in the world of business will do absolute wonders for you and everyone else connected with you!

Remember: Action Cards should *always* be used in a Win-to-the-Winth-Power way and never as a form of manipulation or blackmail, or in other negative or perverse ways, as the currency of money has often been used.

As noted, Action Cards are meant to played, not collected. Life happens right now, so why hold on to them and keep waiting? We're not talking about calculated waiting, where you hang on to your Action Cards because you know that in three turns the payoff will be even better than what's possible now. We mean those who wait for the sake of waiting, or network for the sake of networking, such as people who connect on LinkedIn to anyone and anything in case one day they'll need the connection. Don't stockpile people or Action Cards for some vague right moment. Right now is the right moment, so play what you've got when you got it.

Choose to create the environment of generosity and reciprocity with Action Cards, and just like Phillip McKenzie and Jon Levy, watch how many doors open for you and everyone else involved. After all, this is the New Shared Economy and it's thrilling to be part of it!

# 6 Green Titles and Red Titles

*When I'm old and dying, I plan to look back on my life and say "Wow, that was an adventure," not "Wow, I sure felt safe."*

—Tom Preston-Werner, GitHub cofounder

**Figure 6.1**   Lauren Shapiro Sachs

The uniqueness of the New Entrepreneurz mind-set compared with that of any other is its mastery in turning red titles into green titles.

It's important to note that when we refer to green and red titles, we don't mean shoulds and should nots or dos and don'ts. Should and shouldn'ts are feelings of guilt one experiences because of an imagined gap between some ideal sense of what life should be and what life actually is, whereas dos and don'ts are commands. Neither of those are what we mean.

Neither do green and red titles equate with red lights and green lights. Typically a red light has you stop in your tracks, but green lights mean go, go, go full speed ahead. That's not what we mean, either.

In FreshBiz terminology and in the FreshBiz game, green titles are optional and red titles are mandatory. Here's what we mean:

As you move around the FreshBiz board on your way to winning, above each square is either a green or a red title that applies to the player standing on that square. Because the game is multidimensional, the red or green title is activated *in addition* to the player being able to build a business, take out a loan, leverage the business opportunity, play an Action Card, and more.

It could be that the mandatory red title above the square you've just landed on requires that you pay $1 million to the bank. It could be that the red title indicates you must collect double profits on a business that you built there. Meanwhile, green titles are optional choices. The green title may show that you can play the stock market, sell a business, or collect a million dollars. But it's your choice. Who wouldn't want to collect a million bucks, right? But just as people miss things in life, people miss them in the game, too.

Each green title offers a choice that unlocks a whole new set of possibilities. You are the activator of that green title journey. You probably have no idea how it'll play out in the short term, or the long term, but it's an electric experience to activate new people and connections, new educational streams, and new businesses simply because you view them as available green titles.

In other words, green titles mean "I can." Sometimes you might and sometimes you might not activate them, but you always get to experience the power of it being your choice.

On the other hand, red titles are mandatory actions. You *must* fulfill what is required. Let's put that in a more empowering and inspiring way: Red titles are actions you must choose to do.

As in real life, you can be as creative relative to this as you want. Paying taxes, for example, is a red title, a must. Of course, with some entrepreneurial thinking, you can create tax shelters through investing, giving to a charity, setting up a foundation, and more. You may pay fewer taxes or greater taxes, but paying tax is a red title.

Interestingly enough, we've been raised in a world of too many self-imposed red titles that came along with our inherited belief systems. Here are some of the red titles we often hear about:

- You must go to school.
- You must go to college.
- You must get a good job.
- You must make a lot of money to really matter.
- You must get married and have a family.
- You must have lots of stuff.
- You must work until retirement age.

Too many of us find we're going through life blindly adhering to mandatory red titles. At some point we end up feeling that we've never done anything except what *they* told us we must. Know someone who feels like that?

We sure do! We've both been there before, undergoing our own personal processes of zooming out and letting go of limiting beliefs so that we may live a life of freedom, power, and choice.

## The Lifestyle of the New Entrepreneurz

For decades, the mind-set was to follow blindly in the footsteps of inherited red titles that promised a better future if you locked into them. We view these followers as the "victims of must." How sad that their experience of life is not one of endless choices but a series of mandatory musts. After years and years of this pervasive method, people have started removing their distorted rose-colored glasses, which turned everything into a red title. People are realizing that like roses, rose-colored glasses come with some nasty not-too-rosy thorns. Especially today, when life is so dynamic, choosing to stick to a red title is as crazy as choosing to stay in quicksand.

Green titles are flexible and fluid, like the mind-set of the New Entrepreneurz. They let New Entrepreneurz color outside the lines with as much freedom as they can color inside the lines. What's really fun is that when you become a New Entrepreneur, you feel as though you've picked up a gigantic can of green paint and a huge fluffy paintbrush as you go from place to place, painting red titles green!

Ronen chose to paint the red title of college education into a green one (a few times) when he dropped out and realized it wasn't for him. It's not that he had anything against higher education. It's great for some people. To this day, he really enjoys running FreshBiz workshops for students in higher education programs around the world and recently addressed 50 graduating Harvard MBA students who came to Israel to learn about entrepreneurial thinking from local celebrities in the StartupNation.

But here's the thing: A college or university education is no longer a red title. "You *must* have a degree" doesn't hold anymore because a degree no longer promises what it did a century ago. Today a college education is a green title, a choice, another option in the sea of multiple streams of education open to us. You can work with some amazing companies, start incredible businesses, and connect with some generous or brilliant people regardless of whether you have a degree.

Peter Thiel, the brilliant entrepreneur who cofounded PayPal, owns 10 percent of Facebook, and is a billionaire, has generated attention lately by establishing the Thiel Fellowship. Each year, he awards $100,000 to 20 people younger than 20 years old to drop out of their usually Ivy League universities and pursue their own entrepreneurial ventures. That's right! The world is getting really cool, and there is no shortage of cool programs out there committed to turning the red title of degrees and diplomas into a green title.

It's definitely true that some occupations do require a traditional education. We're pretty sure we'd all want our family doctor to have gone through *all* seven years of medical school and put that knowledge into initially supervised practice, unless, of course, he's Akrit Jaswal, who performed his first surgery at age seven! We would certainly like to work with a seasoned, qualified lawyer, unless, of course, she's Gabrielle Turnquest, the youngest person to pass the UK bar exam! In general, though, certification is needed for some professions, but we highly recommend not relying on only one source for education. A doctor with no holistic mind-body approach, knowledge of Chinese medicine, or knowledge of how important diet is to health, is someone whose medical education, in our view, is still incomplete.

But beyond several professions that do need a university education, we find umpteen students seeking no more than a low-level diploma. This student body, which makes up the majority of students, doesn't really care about the studies but still attends various colleges and institutes because someone said they ought to get a diploma. These students have been convinced by the lie that they'll be ignorant and unattractive job candidates if they don't have a degree. Many are spending tens if not hundreds of thousands of dollars that they often don't have because someone that they trust has done them the disservice of pretending that a university education is a red title.

## Meet Victoria

After running our Win to the Winth Power workshop for 100 students and professors at New York's Pace University, Victoria, a vivacious 21-year-old student, shared with us something that we unfortunately hear all too often. Even though she is an extremely talented dancer with years of experience and a passion for making it her career, she listened to her parents and has spent the past four years getting a college diploma to fall back on. Isn't that crazy?! Spending four or five years on a possible plan B because she was too gentle to face her parents who, perhaps unintentionally, actually sold her the idea that what she wanted to be is not good enough but that she will become good enough if she has the approval of a diploma.

What possibilities might have opened up for Victoria, had she spent one or two years of the time she was blindly spending on college to invest in herself instead, taking the best classes in dance and self-development, acquiring the right mentors and instructors, making powerful connections, and even traveling for different dance opportunities around the world? As we see it, diplomas truly aren't needed for everything. When people tell us they've been attending a university for four, six, or even eight years, we like to get them thinking by asking what else they're doing as their plan B.

Ronen recalls the restaurant in a Tuscany village where he and his wife ate on their honeymoon. They'd just finished eating the most unbelievably delicious Italian cuisine they had ever tasted, and they asked the chef about the school where he learned how to cook and bake. The chef gave a hearty laugh and said, "I learned from life . . . by trial and error, and good mentors."

Here's a thought: Have you ever seen diplomas hanging on museum walls that show paintings by Van Gogh, Monet, or Cezanne, who actually failed the entrance exam for the top Paris art school of the time? Of course not, because who cares? We are inspired by their work, not by their credentials, and their work is what lets us experience the magic of their self-expression and enjoy what they have brought into the world.

This isn't only true for the highly artistic and the supertalented. It's true, currently, for almost everyone, from programmers to teachers, from bank managers to real estate agents, all of whom are creating more green titles, more options, for life and living. Hello, New Entrepreneurz!

Another red title that Ronen was privileged to paint green was the "own a house" title. If you're married with children, owning a house is the secure, responsible thing an adult does. Of course, once you've managed to buy that house, you definitely don't sell it except to move to a better house, right? This is probably one of the most expensive red titles out there because we're raised from an early age to believe that the house is where the home is, where you raise your family, where you live your life, and where you spend your days. It's the core. It stands for safety and security. It's the fulfillment of a dream.

Pressure, presented as commonsense, starts early. This is what we *didn't* hear our parents saying: "Oh, you're only 25! Take some time to discover the secrets of the world, fall in love, explore your passions, invest in yourself, start a business, learn lessons, pay some rent but be mobile, and then in 25 or 30 years you'll be in a great position to buy a nice house, fully paid in cash, and live peacefully ever after."

Yeah, right!

It usually sounds more like this: "Oh dear, time's literally flying by, and you'll be old before you know it. You need to buckle down, be responsible, and start thinking about your future, because we won't always be here for you. Stop playing games, get a diploma, find a good job, buy a starter house, and start making those mortgage payments, so in 30 years from now, if your life is a train wreck, at least you'll own your own home."

As Ronen mentioned in the opening chapter, he chose to invest in himself instead of investing in the bank and the real estate market. That's because he believed doing that was a better investment. He took his paintbrush and painted green all over this red title. Just to clarify, we have nothing against home ownership, but it should be linked to choice, self-expression, and the best timing for each person.

Home ownership and its white picket fence should not be portrayed in a way that turns it into a red title.

## Back in the New York City Days

When it comes to being self-employed, which Simcha has been since his early 20s, there can be waves of ups and downs. Paychecks don't necessarily turn up weekly. Sometimes they don't come at all, and sometimes they come so heavily and so happily that it seems there will never be a dry season again—until there is. During the time spent living in New York and running their own marketing company, Simcha and his wife learned to lean on credit cards for personal and business expenses when things got too heavy. One specific year as new young managers was so challenging that they found themselves playing the balance transfer game with a little more than $40,000 of credit card debt. What a source of frustration and discomfort both for their business and for their marriage.

Three years into running their business, they qualified for a $40,000 Super Bonus. Most managers use it toward buying a property or traveling, but Simcha and his wife put that hard-earned money to pay their debts to get back to a healthy zero. Friends and family attending the flashy event, where a massive cardboard check was awarded and loads of photos were taken, thought the young couple's lives would now be perfect. After all, now they were loaded! Of course, as young New Yorkers wrapped up in the prestige of it all, Simcha and his wife didn't have the heart to tell them where the money really went.

## Is Plastic Surgery Good for You?

Author, radio personality, and dynamo Dave Ramsey tirelessly works to help America get out of debt through a method he calls plastic surgery. It involves cutting up your credit cards and taking the *seven baby steps,* the first of which is setting up an emergency fund of $1,000 cash. He's an awesome human being on a mission. His radio show and books, such as *Total Money Makeover, Financial Peace,* and *Entre-Leadership,* are guiding lights to many of Simcha's family and friends. Dave's sage advice and teachings, not to mention the young couple's personal debt history, caused them to color credit cards as a red title: "You must not use credit cards."

It took Simcha and his wife a good deal of reading, processing, and comprehension to transform that red title into a green title known as "helpful credit card." Through smart and responsible spending, which is paid back monthly, credit cards allow Simcha's family and partners to earn a currency of miles and points that turn into free flights and hotels. Thank you, Dansdeals.com, for being an incredible place to learn this new game with all its tricks, its nuances, and the latest information. It is fun having great places to go and being able to do so with little to no money. Hmm, now how can we redeem miles and points for another can of green paint?

## Do People Prefer Red?

Reality shows something fascinating; often people tend to switch things automatically into red titles because they prefer it like that! That's because red titles are actually so much easier to handle. There is no reason to be creative or proactive when backed into a corner. A clear delineation in the form of *must* or *must not* means the individual isn't required to think too deeply. That in turn allows the person to feel forced into an action, which in turn promotes the thought pattern that because the action is coerced rather than a choice, he or she is not responsible for its outcome. "Get a job" is a red title that has many believing it's mandatory to get a job. Everyone's seeking a job, hoping or praying for a job, or looking to the government to hand out jobs. All these people are judging themselves and the value of their lives based on whether they have a job rather than choosing to be creative in procuring meaningful and productive work.

## The Red Title of Wellness

Red titles also get dragged into the health and wellness spheres of our lives. Diets often fail because they require slapping a red title on so many foods that people can't maintain the musts and must nots. Once people break a diet, there's a wave of guilt. Instead of immediately going back to healthy food, exercise, good sleep, and meditation, they binge and basically self-destruct. Here's a fabulous health and wellness green title anecdote.

Tony Robbins, one of the greatest leaders of self-development who explores human success behaviors, tells a story about his wife, Sage. Both Tony and Sage are committed to health and nutritious eating. So Tony was shocked when Sage ordered a rich, creamy milkshake on their first date. "I thought you were into health?" Tony asked. Sage's wise response was along the lines of "I am, but you can still live a bit, too!" Make health a green title by choice.

## Red and Green Titles and College Student Summer Jobs

Often, students view being a camp counselor, a sales clerk, or a lifeguard or working in the supermarket as red titled student jobs essential for funding school. But when you realize that it's not about the job but rather about the experience and making money, green titles open up everywhere!

Look at these, for example: Dave Ramsey tells the story of the daughter of one of his radio show callers who spent the summer researching and filling out close to 1,000 scholarship applications. She was rejected by more than 970 of them, but what she qualified for brought in close to $30,000. Not bad for flexible work done over just one summer! In our seminars, we have met a 12-year-old who bought and sold on eBay and made more than his 17-year-old brother working all summer as a counselor, a 19-year-old freelancer with a full-time income from pursuing her love of designing logos on Fiverr, and another fun artsy student with an amazingly successful business on Etsy that allows him to do what he loves and monetize it while going to school, without being strapped for cash. If you are a student or your child is a student, don't feel locked into the red title known as "student job." Take advantage of the endless resources available that make working smart very rewarding.

Go, green titles, go!

## Red to Green How-To

What process do the New Entrepreneurz use to magically turn red titles into green ones? It starts with zooming out and asking a question. Zooming out always creates an expanded space that enables a new or refreshed possibility for seeing things. Here are some of the questions to ask yourself:

1. Is this really a red title? In other words, am I really in a "must or must not do" status relative to this situation? Tip: Don't confuse this with "Is it easier for me to see it as a red title?"

2. Could there be a scenario where this is not the case?

3. What options or other choices can I think of besides this? Tip: Go online and see how other people are handling the situation. Because we can tap into the world's body of knowledge, experiences, and opinions, it makes for a wealth of new ideas on what else is possible.

Know that you are capable and smart enough to see more green titles in your life. It's no longer about you being the expert. You can research and find an expert online and choose successfully. Know that the red titles in your life are often subjective red titles, rather than objective red titles.

## Coaching Turns Red Titles into Green Titles

In our world, title colors are in our heads. They're a mind-set.

As with *The Matrix,* where some rules can be bent and some, broken, very few red titles are mandatory according to law, ethics, or morals. Challenging red titles are generally linked to jobs, relationships, money, down time, and schooling. These are areas in which we set the rules, and if we're making the rules, then we're entitled to change them or change how we think about those rules.

This is precisely where coaching and consciousness come into play. All your musts and must nots are beliefs that color the titles "Get a job," "I only like tall men," "I must go to school," and many more. Seek a mentor, find a coach, invest in a seminar or workshop that will help you shift how you see things, and most important, be on a mission to grow beyond your set beliefs.

Always keep in mind that everything you've been taught to be true is really someone else's game of red and green titles. You own the right to play your own game. It's our mission to help you see more green titles around you as well as turn more of your red titles into green ones.

The process of becoming part of the tribe of New Entrepreneurz is the process of turning those red titles into green titles. The more beliefs you turn, the more freedom and choice you have in your life.

So grab your paint cans and let's paint the town *green!*

# 7 Smart Business

*Chase the vision, not the money; the money will end up following you.*

—Tony Hsieh, Zappos chief executive officer

**Figure 7.1**   Stefanie Diamond

I t's almost like we forgot that our mission is to bring value to those who are looking for it. It's not a war to win but rather a light to be shone.

We've gotten ready, and we've gotten set; now it's time to get into action. It's playtime! As we've discussed in the previous chapters, the world is dynamic and is in a constant state of flux, making it important to learn how to generate change. We specifically say *generate*, because it comes from within rather than from without. Generating change means that instead of waiting for something to happen, you choose to create proactively. Participants of our game-based FreshBiz curriculum frequently note how one of their keenest insights is that "Life doesn't take turns, so you need to play what you've got when you got it!"

So now it's time to do something different. No more thinking about things, pontificating, being cerebral, or discussing theory. Now it's time to take actions that create ripples in the real world. It's time to bring the New Entrepreneurz mind-set and tools into real-life action by creating a smart business. We'll be talking about smart businesses, but the principles remain the same for turning anything into a smart venture, whether it's in the realm of relationships, of creating a new school, or even of planning a vacation.

## Smart Business 101

*Smart business* is the approach to business that uses an elevated mind-set and smart tools to engage the ideal customers and deliver your message.

The most common approach toward business stems from two old-system factors: a mind-set centered on competition and a mentality guided by scarcity. Think about how frequently you hear people refer to the competitive job market or talk about how their business could be doing better, with sentences such as, "It's just that there's so much competition out there." These are distorted perceptions people convince themselves to believe, instead of thinking creatively about how they can distinguish themselves, work smarter instead of harder, and leverage more tools to help them win the game. But we've grown so accustomed to using this kind of language that it slips in automatically when we talk about marketing and expanding our business.

How many of these phrases do you instantly recognize, for example?

- Conquering a new market
- Capturing the audience
- Convincing our target demographic
- Beating out the competition
- Taking over the market
- Dominating the market

Are we going to bloody war here, or are we just trying to grow our business?!

Phrases such as these can't help but make us feel as though we're in the dystopian zero-sum Hunger Games. This kind of language arises from a scarcity mind-set, which claims that because there isn't enough for everyone, winning can be achieved only by *annihilating* the *competition*. We pretend it's vital to be strong, tough, manipulative, and cunning—nothing less than an expert hunter/warrior. But the truth is that this kind of mentality doesn't resonate with most people at the emotional level. It's something that they have to put on, much like a costume or better yet, protective armor, as they head into imaginary battles. It's an attitude that certainly doesn't resonate with the Millennials and the New Entrepreneurz who are building and creating new companies from a socially conscious place of authenticity and radical transparency.

A smart business is built on abundance and collaboration, not suit-and-tie wars and competitions. Humans naturally want to help others, and now we can. It's time to let go of the illusion of competition and focus on how to run a smart, successful business that matches each of us best.

## Packaging a Value

There are more people in the world than your business can ever serve, so focus on sharing your unique voice to attract the right ones.

When you truly understand that your market is endless because, on a global level, you can never serve everyone, then the game of smarketing becomes packaging the right value for the right people.

Your job as a New Entrepreneur is simply to package value in the form of products and services and then help the right people find out about it.

It sounds simple, and yet many entrepreneurs and business executives tend to lose sight of this simple concept as they grow their businesses. They start with a novel idea for something that can bring value to themselves, their friends, or potential customers and then build a product or service around it. At a certain point, they get lost or distracted and instead of continuing to create new value through evolving, they start focusing on expanding, which we believe is the incorrect direction to take. One example would be a company that, instead of choosing to improve the product, focuses on opening numerous new branches or shifts from offering extraordinary service to cost-effective service. Once the business begins its pursuit of *more* instead of *better,* it slowly kills off the smart business core.

Sometimes it can be difficult to differentiate between evolving and expanding. Let's look at Facebook's acquisition of WhatsApp for $19 billion. Facebook now controls more information and transactions, but is that evolving or expanding? The answer depends on how Facebook handles WhatsApp. If it's used to charge money from advertisers without providing better engagement for advertisers and users, then that is simply expanding. It brings value only to stockholders while reducing value for billions of users. But if Facebook uses this purchase to enhance everyone's social experience and indeed "make the world more open and connected," as Facebook's mission states, then it is staying within its mission and is therefore evolving.

Packaging a value is also a great approach that will help you grow your business without necessarily getting into heavy investments. By listening to your customers and partners and being adaptive, you can create *new* and exciting products that will deliver a *lot* of value to your customers.

## Building Your Smart Business

FreshBiz has given us the opportunity to coach, train, or interview thousands of businesses around the globe. Over the past few years of learning and understanding what constitutes the essence of a smart business, we've identified what we consider the three defining elements. To make them more effective for you, the reader, we've included some additional tips and tricks to help you enhance your business today!

The three characteristics of a smart business are:

**1.** It serves a higher mission with your unique voice.

**2.** It demonstrates Win to the Winth Power.

**3.** It supports your lifestyle.

## Characteristic 1: Serves a Higher Mission with Your Unique Voice

We've already discussed this in no small amount of detail, so we won't revisit this conversation too deeply. But we do wish to emphasize a couple of points. What do we mean when we refer to a higher mission? Higher than what?

The buzz in the community of New Entrepreneurz is that it's not just important to effect a shift in mind-set but also to elevate that mind-set. We don't necessarily mean something of epic proportions. Napoleon Hill, the author of *Think and*

*Grow Rich,* says it best: "If you can't do great things, do small things in a great way."

A higher mission doesn't have to aim at changing the entire world. It could be something that changes some people's world. Also, it doesn't have to change the world completely; it just needs to make a significant difference, or as they say in the world of self-development, it needs to "make a difference that makes a difference." The best way to know if you make a difference is by asking yourself a simple but profound question: "Will I be missed?" In other words, if you were to close your business or not show up to work tomorrow, who would miss you?

A great example of such a business is a special boutique women's club in Tel Aviv, Israel, called 9 Rooms. Although we're men, we were privileged to be given a special behind-the-scenes tour by its founder, Iris Zohar. (Learn more about Iris in the Interviews section at the back of the book.) As she hosted us in her magnificent space and we were served tea and cookies, she shared her beautifully phrased mission: to give each and every member the privilege of being treated like a queen for a few hours every week. Serving this mission, she believes, has a ripple effect across many lives and many families.

We certainly know that taking care of our wives, female entrepreneurs, and our kids' moms, educators, and nurturers is crucial and that they're certainly deserving of special care, but we might not always know how best to go about it. Iris made it easy by creating a sacred space of pampering that makes a multidimensional difference when we think of all the worlds that our talented ladies juggle in life. This is the role that Iris chooses to play through her vehicle known as 9 Rooms. We highly recommend signing up; either when a local chapter in your city opens up, or on your next trip to the StartupNation. Women only, of course! Be sure you're invited when you visit Tel Aviv so that you can experience what doing small things in a great way really looks and feels like. The welcome smile, the drinks, the facials, the content lectures, the food, and the music—are all planned down to the most minute details to take you on a regal journey.

## Tips and Tricks

In the famous TED Talk that all new businesses are talking about, Simon Sinek profoundly shares that people don't buy *what* you do; they buy into *why* you do it. Simply put, the motive and story behind what you're doing is the most important thing to share and to encourage others to share. Think about it: Nowadays many of us find ourselves caring more about the people driving the businesses than the businesses themselves. This is because a lot of the new successful companies are actually a unique expression of their owner's voice, and the New Entrepreneurz find that fascinating!

### *Consider the Preexit Strategy and the $25,000 Question*

The best tip we can give you to determine whether your business is purpose-driven is the preexit strategy and the $25,000 question. Imagine that your closest friend lays down $25,000 on the table and offers it to you in exchange for never ever pursuing and monetizing that amazing idea you have. Would you take it?

If you do take it, it's an indication that you wanted to build the business for the wrong reason: just to make money. This is not really the business you would want to build. Nowadays, people build businesses for much better reasons than just money: as an avenue of self-expression, to answer their calling, to solve a problem, to be a guiding light, and more.

But if you choose not to take it, to just say no to your friend's lousy $25,000 offer, because your idea is worth more than that and worth everything to you, then *that* is a business worth building. The $25,000 question also helps you define your unique position in the business by allowing you to identify which elements are unique to you and close to your heart. So, for example, if you have a Web-building studio, you might choose to give up the search engine optimization (SEO) department, but you'll never give up design, because design expresses your essence.

**Communicate Your Mission, Not Your Products**   We come across a lot of business owners who express concern that they have nothing unique to share because they have a regular profession: real estate agent, lawyer, or accountant, for example. But don't make the mistake of thinking you have nothing to say—because you do!

Regardless of your business, product, or service, think about the various messages you can already share with people about your specific expertise by simply taking a step back. By looking at the deeper level of *why* you do what you do, and *why you* specifically, you are already shining the spotlight on what you can communicate and how you can give value to people even before any monetary transaction takes place.

Any business can easily put together a blog or assemble some amazing images on Instagram or Pinterest telling its unique story. A great idea that we came across on the blog of Tim Ferris, *The 4-Hour Work Week,* involves creating five simple tutorials a week on how to do something related to your business. After 10 weeks you would have 50 individual roads leading back to you, which would translate into thousands of extra dollars each month, for providing good value in your field. If you're thinking, "How would I come up with so much to say?" it isn't difficult when you reflect on how much you know about any given topic in your field.

For example, if you are a real estate agent, you can come up with at least five tutorials about making your house easy to sell, what to look for when buying a property, or how to buy a house with no initial funds. But let's look at someone whom the entrepreneurial community knows very well: the successful and outspoken Gary Vaynerchuk.

Gary's family winery was one of many in California, without much to make it stand out. Realizing the opportunity to not only talk about the family winery but also talk about wines in general, Gary took over the marketing for his family business and, through his daily wine video blog, transformed it from a $3 million to a $45 million business. What did he do? He created *Wine Library TV,* which introduced new, exciting wines—including some from his so-called competitors—to viewers every day to help expand their palate. After 1,000 episodes, he had not only reached more than 100,000 viewers daily but also used the *Wine Library TV* platform to launch his career as a best-selling author and marketing entrepreneur, speaking at events worldwide.

Gary did it, and each and every one of us can also find our unique message and media channel to convey it.

**Build a Tribe**  The best way to see whether you are doing a great job is to check and see how your customers view themselves. Are they customers or community members? Seth Godin, in his best seller titled *Tribes: We Need You to Lead Us,* talks about the importance of building a tribe. Basically that means how to turn customers into actively engaged community members. It's amazing, but one of the things we notice and really appreciate is that no matter where we go in the world, our FreshBiz tribe members, known as FreshBizers, never feel just like customers. Whether they buy a game, a workshop, or whatever else, they tell us how they feel and experience being part of the movement itself. The best practices we found for engaging our FreshBizers are the following three actions:

1. Let your tribe members become part of the way you deliver the message by treating them as partners and cocreators of the products and services.

2. Set up *communitycation!* In other words, communicate directly with your community and let them communicate with each other. When engaged in the same mind-set

rhythm as others around you, your communication and community become transformational. So be sure to give them a platform where they can communicate among themselves. It's not a community if only you talk to them and, at the most, they can respond to you. Becoming a community means engaging with similarly involved people. Although it's pretty easy to supply a technical platform for this, such as Facebook groups or forums, the challenge is to let go of your full control over the conversation and place your trust in your tribe.

3. Provide easy-to-use tools that let them proudly share their message within yours. Many tribe members will like your product or service enough to share it with others but lack the right tools to do so. It's your responsibility to provide your tribe with easy-to-use, engaging tools that make it simple to share the message.

One example is a simple service we created for use in our workshops, called The Share Game. Workshop participants can sign in on their smartphones during the break, sharing their experiences live on Facebook, and an automatic link for the next workshop's registration is attached to their posts. All participants who shared their experience are entered in our on-the-spot raffle to win a $1,000 seminar. We receive many, many clicks on those shared experiences and literally everyone wins!

Putting these few simple steps into action will already frame your business the right way and attract the right people to be part of your community.

## Characteristic 2: Demonstrates Win to the Winth Power

Meeting your higher mission is a great thing, but it must also be aligned with other people meeting their higher missions as well. As smart businesses we need to empower and inspire each other so that we can truly become the critical mass needed to completely transform the face of business. Demonstrating Win to the Winth Power is the way to do it. Putting this concept into action may take the form of creating a smartnership business model for your company, providing a creative work environment for your team, designing ecofriendly products, or structuring a lean business to save on resources. A combination of more than one of these is always welcome, too!

A GameChangers 500 company and a great example of a business built on Win to the Winth Power is 2 Degrees Food. The company uses the one-for-one model that TOMS uses for shoes and Warby Parker uses for glasses, but 2 Degrees Food applies it to a good people buy way more often: food. Not just any food, but tasty, nutritious food. In case you're not familiar with the one-for-one model, it operates very simply: For every item you purchase, the company gives another away for free to someone who really needs it and can't afford it. In the first two years of operations selling 2 Degrees Food healthy snack bars, the company donated more than a million meals to hungry children around the world, based on a simple formula: One bar = one meal. Lauren Walters, the company's founder, shared with us that when people are given a choice and a chance to affect the world positively, they will take it. (Learn more about Lauren in the Interviews section at the back of the book.) 2 Degrees Food created an easy platform in the form of a healthy snack bar that people can buy several times a day. Each purchase leads to a free meal for a hungry child in the world. The customer can even choose where the meal goes.

That's an impressive example of implementing Win to the Winth Power in a business model. For 2 Degrees Food the bar is only the start of an ever-expanding mission focused on inspiring others to implement the one-for-one model across all food products in the world. Imagine if whatever you bought was then matched with another one like it going to someone else who really needs it. This is a smart business!

## Tips and Tricks

Because Win to the Winth Power is essentially multidimensional winning, you must first start by understanding and evaluating the different dimensions of your game. For some businesses, being ecofriendly might be the dimension of most importance, whereas moms running start-ups might consider the dimension of family time the most central. The moment you begin to focus on the dimensions of importance to you and the people around you is the moment when you can begin working smart to figure out the best way to synthesize them.

***Find Partners for Success*** Communicate your different dimensions rather than just your business goals.

Business goals tend mostly to be monetary, but it's time to move ahead to a deeper level of communication that takes into consideration other elements as well. This activates and powers multiple ways for people to engage in your success and for you to engage in theirs.

Create an interest for other people to be invested in your success. Different people have different levels of interest in your success, and it isn't always money related. Obviously, your mom and dad are invested in a different way than your community members or your banker.

So here is an easy exercise to find partners for success: Make a list of 15 people in your life who may have an interest in what you're doing. Write down:

**1.** The names

**2.** The specific interests they could have in your business

**3.** Action items to communicate to them

It should look something like this:

Step 1: Mom and Dad

Step 2: They would love for me to be able to do what I love and provide for my family while doing it.

Step 3: They have the ability to support me by babysitting the kids so that I can put more time into my new business. I should sit down with them and give a better explanation on how an extra afternoon with the grandkids can really help me run meetings outside the city and enlarge the business.

It could also look like this:

Step 1: My banker

Step 2: He wants me to make more money so that I can pay back my loans and take advantage of additional bank services.

Step 3: Ask him to invite other bank customers to the workshops I run. This adds value to his customers and helps them make more money, too, while allowing me to bring in additional revenue. I can set a meeting with the banker, explain the value of my workshops, and give him invitations that will make him and the bank look good.

**Create Win-to-the-Winth-Power Partnerships** A more streamlined term we've come up with for this type of collaboration is *smartnerships,* smart partnerships that allow everyone to benefit and expand each other's incomes and outcomes by working together.

Here are some ways to achieve that. Some businesses have begun making their employees co-owners in the company: Instead of earning an hourly rate only, these employees become integrated into the macro. Similarly, 2 Degrees Food creates partners out of its customers by actively involving them in fulfilling its vision.

**See Who Is in Your Business Economy** The way to build smart partnerships is to zoom out from what you're doing and take a full look at the entire economy of your business. In other words, you need to look not only at the income you personally make, or that your company makes, but also at all incomes generated from everyone you affect. Let's say, for example, that you're a graphic designer: Your business is actually affecting a lot of other businesses as well because part of your work includes other businesses, such as photographers, fashion stylists, Web programmers, printers, and more. So, while you may make $10,000 a month, your economy might be making $50,000 a month in total. You should view this total as part of your business because it's generated as part of your efforts. This makes your community of partners larger than you thought and allows you to leverage like a business that generates $50,000 instead of just $10,000. Now you can start playing a bigger game by inviting your partners to take an active role in growing your communal economy even more.

Here's a four-step approach on how to do that:

1. Make a list of everyone who benefits from your business. The list should include suppliers, customers, distributors, facilitators, salespeople, and any other relevant companies or persons. View everyone as a potential partner. So your supplier is no longer your supplier but your *partner* who supplies what you need.

2. Make a list of five Action Cards each of these partners holds that can advance your business: for example, their community e-mail lists, customers, connections, venues, and knowledge.

**3.** Price your partners' profits; estimate how much they earn (in dollars and in other currencies as well) because of your relationship.

**4.** Sit together and look for ways to expand the profits pie by now leveraging the entire collection of Action Cards.

Here's an example: You, the friendly graphic designer we mentioned before, identify your photographer as part of your total business economy. Whenever she gets a gig from you, she makes around $1,000 for her photography services. You take a deeper look at her Action Cards and discover that she has a photography blog with 5,000 followers. This is a powerful resource for you to leverage in reaching some amazing potential customers.

You calculate that she makes around $9,000 a year from your business and referrals, so you sit together to create ways of doubling or tripling that. You ask for a featured spot on the blog, which means every month, she will feature you with a blog post about graphic design, branding, or life design. In return, you will promote her as your photographer for any future lead work that will be generated from her followers reaching you from the new posts.

Together you just expanded the pie chart for potential revenues and customers.

Now, just imagine doing this with 7 or 10 of your economy partners. This example is based on a true story, and we know for a fact that it generated thousands of extra dollars in revenues for all parties involved.

## *Turn Challenges into Win-to-the-Winth-Power Experiences*

When you keep your eyes open and your mind-set tuned, then even the craziest challenges can turn into a Win-to-the-Winth-Power experience.

Our facilitators' community is awesome. We'll never forget when our FreshBiz partners in Russia told us about a really important workshop they were running for a major consulting company looking to experience gamification and entrepreneurial development. The only challenge was that with less than five days to go, it seemed our games were still stuck at Customs and wouldn't be released for weeks. After some beers, a game of FreshBiz, and a walk on the beach, we came up with our crazy idea for a solution. Within 10 minutes we'd already advertised on our Facebook group of FreshBiz facilitators, offering a free round-trip flight to Moscow plus a two-night stay for leaving the following evening with 10 FreshBiz games in his or her suitcase to save the day for our Russian partners. Of course, because she's a FreshBizer, a facilitator named Shiran wrote back less than 2 minutes later to say she was in!

She left as planned, had a fun experience, took amazing Instagram photos at the Kremlin, and had even more proof that she lives the awesome lifestyle of the New Entrepreneurz. She shared with us how exciting it was when this spontaneous opportunity popped up on her smartphone. Because she has always wanted to go to Russia, and was looking for a fresh experience for her blog, she took the opportunity and had a blast.

Behind the scenes, our thought process was simple. First, we defined the challenge and asked ourselves how we could win the game, which in this case meant getting the FreshBiz games to Russia for workshop participants signed up for the event just days away. Then we looked at the gap between the current situation and the obvious solution and found that no delivery service could handle our requirement that quickly, and none of the founding partners were available. We then expanded our thinking, looked into other resources, and reevaluated who else could be a partner in providing the solution. After all, we had the games, we had the budget, and we had our community. The missing step was how to create a great story and an awesome experience that would go beyond merely solving the problem.

So we ended up turning a delivery task into a free vacation opportunity that left our Russian business center deeply moved by our commitment, turned a workshop into a great success with repeat business, and inspired the heck out of our community through their hearing this story and seeing Shiran's incredible pictures and new blog entry.

## Characteristic 3: Supports Your Lifestyle

A smart business is a sustainable one. For it to last long term without crashing and burning, it has to support your lifestyle and align with what you consider important values and quality of life. For one person that may look like working only four days a week or getting to travel the world, and for someone else it might mean supplying employment for thousands of people in a cool culture and affecting local communities. So how do you know if your business supports your lifestyle?

L. P. Jacks is famous for his quote about the master in the art of living: "The master in the art of living makes little distinction between his work and his play . . . to him he is always doing both." At FreshBiz this is our mantra, and the master in the art of living is our role model.

Our choice of structure for FreshBiz allows us, the founders and partners, to live the lifestyle of storytelling, mind-shifting New Entrepreneurz. What does this mean for us? No office, no office hours, frequent traveling, story hunting, no employees, fluidity, staying dynamic, being flexible, and choosing constant growth through the endeavors and challenges we accept, while ensuring quality time with our families to nurture our home lives. When we were invited by Indian Institute of Technology Bombay to take part in its 2013 annual e-summit entrepreneurship weekend, it took us less than an hour to get back to the school with a yes, even though it would bring in only a few thousand dollars in revenue. We chose to turn this opportunity into a full partners' journey to India. It was a perfect fit for our FreshBiz lifestyle of traveling, meeting and affecting new cultures, and having some fun while doing it.

In addition to running our game-based workshops, which in and of itself was quite an experience, we were asked to run the "scaling-up challenge" to a packed room of more than 100 business students. Typically in all the articles we read on Flipboard, LinkedIn, StumbleUpon, and others, scaling-up challenges in most companies tend to deal with manufacturing, storage, marketing, delivery—all that boring stuff. We wanted to have fun, rock the boat, and challenge them with a new way of thinking about lifestyle-based scaling up in business.

We presented them with our personal challenge: How can we be a $10 million-a-year company without ending up working in an office? After a couple of minutes of stunned silence filling the room, the students set to work and started asking the right questions, which ultimately turned into more than 50 pages' worth of ideas and thoughts about how to face that challenge. It was a great opportunity to learn from each other while emphasizing the aspect of how we see the *future* of business, *today*.

As an aside, leveraging this event created an opportunity to spend some great quality time with our local Indian partners drinking fresh coconut milk, riding around in rickshaws, partying in Bangalore, enjoying the spa, telling our story on national TV for an audience of 50 million people, and starting the first India-based FreshBiz business center of Asia.

## Tips and Tricks

The way to support yourself in living the lifestyle you want to live while maintaining a growing, healthy business is by focusing on keeping things lean, looking for leverage, and of course taking care of life outside the business.

There are increasing numbers of articles on life hacking, growth hacking, and business hacking to reveal how we can get more from less. Dive right in and explore how to build a lean business that serves you rather than *you* serving it.

**Build a Lean Business**  A common lifestyle goal we encounter is being able to run your business while exploring the world and still having enough time to engage in other hobbies, values, and activities. Many business owners would love an automated, passive income-generating machine that would keep providing for them even if they took off for a month or two. The lean business is step one toward fulfilling this typical New Entrepreneurz lifestyle wish.

Eric Ries, in his awesome book titled *The Lean Startup*, goes into what this means in full detail, but here's what a lean business means to us. In general it means that you have only the facilities needed to support your business rather than facilities that support your ego. Nowadays with technology and social media you can get so much more for so much less. This makes the business requirements we were used to, such as office space, secretaries, employees, infrastructures, and software, no longer as essential to running your business.

We already discussed the New Shared Economy in depth, so here is a tool on how to use it to create your lean business. Make a list of all the facilities you might need for your business. Everyone's buzzing about how access trumps ownership so find areas where *you* can choose access over ownership.

To get you started, it should look something like this:

| Facility | Ownership | Access |
|---|---|---|
| Office space | Buy or rent an office | Use a shared working space or work from home or a coffee shop |
| Car | Buy a car | Rent a car per hour/day, bike, use ride sharing |
| Secretary | Employee | Virtual assistant, make your own coffee and type your own letters (filing days are over), Fiverr gigs |
| IT services | Employees, hardware | Dropbox, Google Drive, Elance |
| Team | Employees | Smartnerships, internpreneurs |
| Storage and delivery | Storage space, employees | Amazon.com fulfillment center, print on demand |

By replacing some of the old resources with access rather than ownership, you reduce costs and headaches and create more speed, flexibility, and leverage. And again, for more resources check out life hacking, business hacking, and growth hacking tips and groups online, which let you go further with less.

**Work on Your Business Instead of in It** Bill Gates was famous for taking a few weeks off from working at Microsoft and going away somewhere to recalibrate. Being freed up from the day-to-day responsibilities allowed the space to conduct a thorough holistic overview of the business and make smart moves. After all, a minor tweak in the macro creates a major tweak to the micro. Breaks like these allowed him to return and execute powerful decisions that moved the business forward in the direction it needed. The trick to working on your business is actually taking time off from your business, not just for 15 minutes here and 25 minutes there. Learn to allow yourself time away from your business and away from home, too, on occasion, so that you can identify the optimal solutions.

Don't ever be so busy working hard that you forget to work smart. It's so easy to find yourself locking into doing more of the same. Time away breaks up a stale rhythm and allows for a complete refresh, which helps you get back on track.

Here are some ideas on how to spend your time working *on* your business.

Ask questions about:

- How to improve your customers' experience
- How to create leverage in your business
- What new smartnerships can be created
- What are some new ideas for products, services, and marketing campaigns
- How to sharpen your message
- How to set up good communitycation
- Which influencers to connect with
- What raw feedback random customers give
- What other experts in your field say

Last, commit yourself to guaranteeing that your time away will happen. So book your flight; sign up for that full-day seminar; lock in that great hotel or Airbnb home for the weekend; head over to the beach, spa, or coffee shop; and have some fun refreshing yourself!

### *Know That a Real Lifestyle Is Not about Having More; It Is about Becoming More*   Jim Rohn, the father of the personal development industry, said, "Formal education will make you a living; self-education will make you a fortune." At FreshBiz we know that the fortune appears in the form of money, experiences, Action Cards, and lifestyle.

Whether you call it personal development, self-development, or business development, engaging in working to become the best version of yourself as possible, along with others doing the same, makes for extraordinary living. It also creates great returns on investment, so invest in yourself and choose which seminars, workshops, books, or training sessions you'll join over the next quarter. The best way to ensure you're on the path of self-development is to invest more time and money in experiences and knowledge rather than in stuff. Instead of a new pair of shoes, invest in a new book; instead of updating your smartphone for a few hundred bucks, enroll in a game-changing workshop. Sometimes do both! You'll get more from the seminar than from the latest flat screen, we promise.

### *Play the Experience and Self-Development Game*

Step 1: Create for yourself a special PayPal or Amazon account or a special prepaid loadable credit card.

Step 2: Transfer $100 into it, because you're worth it.

Step 3: Every time you pay for stuff (other than food, housing, and bills) transfer between 8 and 20 percent of the purchase figure into that special account. You bought a new smartphone for $500? Put at least $40 into your self-development account.

Step 4: Start using it to unlock experiences, new communities, and yourself.

Bonus step: Because you don't really need all that stuff anyway, just start swapping it directly for experiences and self-development!

**Go from Scaling Up to Scaling Smart** Most businesses focus on scaling up. We see this as a mistake because scaling up has nothing to do with being purpose-driven or supporting your lifestyle. It mostly has to do with old-school, ego-based achievements. We encourage you to start looking at how to scale smart.

By now you already understand that measuring your business based solely on size, real estate, and money has nothing to do with turning your business into a smart business. The reason many businesses still use that old Fortune 500 model as the litmus test to determine whether they are successful is because before now, there really was no alternative model. Businesses used to be measured in terms of small or big. Not anymore. The new model is the smart business. We can't wait to see where you take it. You deserve it!

# 8 All-in

*You jump off a cliff and you assemble an airplane on the way down.*

—Reid Hoffman, LinkedIn cofounder

**Figure 8.1**    Zev Steinhardt

When we think of going all-in, the image of a poker player comes to mind, thrusting all his or her chips into the center of the table, declaring all-in, and waiting for the cards to determine his or her fate.

The truth is that we can go all-in relative to every aspect of our lives. Rather than merely trusting fate but living the right way, going all-in can actually be a healthy, invigorating, and exciting way to live. The all-in mind-set is what enabled Ronen to sell his house for the sake of producing the first thousand games of FreshBiz and realizing his dream, and we'll talk more about that later.

## The New World Mind-Set

The New Entrepreneurz go all-in with what they do. Choosing proactivity, they live life through a prism of being present, conscious, and mindful within the different dimensions of their lives. They don't play small, play it safe, or wait for later. They go all-in with passion, dedication, and drive.

So what ingredient do they have in the mix that others seem to be missing? First and foremost, they understand that going all-in is not *permanent*. A poker player who goes all-in on a hand and loses doesn't abstain from ever playing again. The new mind-set goes all-in for a particular time frame or a specific area of activity, knowing that the decision might work out and might not, but because life itself won't be over, another hand, so to speak, can always be played. This can come in the form of opening a different business, making a new friend, moving to a new city, and so on.

Because you can go all-in again and again, there's no point in holding on to little pockets of artificial scarcity for later.

Go all-in for your own sake. After all, you're worth it.

Too many people think that if going all-in has failed, then their lives are over. But that isn't the case at all! Here's what actually happens:

*You fall, fall, fall, and then learn to stand. Next thing, you're walking.*

*You fall, fall, fall, and then learn to bike. Before you know it, you're driving.*

*You fall, fall, fall . . . next thing you know, you're succeeding in life.*

You can't save getting it right for later. You've got to do your best to be great now so that you wind up in the later of your dreams. So here is the first question you should ask yourself.

## Do You Plan on Going All-in Someday? If So, Why Not Today?

There really is no good reason to wait to execute that business decision, take that online Coursera course, invest more time in your best relationships, or send that InMail on LinkedIn. Don't save that action for later. Don't wait for the perfect constellation to invest your energy. At this very moment, you're the best version of yourself that you can be, so now is the best time.

Knowing this, New Entrepreneurz go all-in in their relationships, business, health, or education activities. That's what makes them so charming and distinguishes them from almost everyone else out there.

Sadly, the reason most people don't become entrepreneurs is because their mind-set is holding them back, pretending that going all-in is unsafe, risky, and dangerous. But New Entrepreneurz really don't see any other way to be, because they understand that going all-in is demonstrating full expression of themselves, and they refuse to be kept on hold.

## The Right Way to Go All-in

We want to be sure we're literally on the same page here as far as the right type of all-in because there are three ways to go all-in:

1. By holding a winning hand
2. By bluffing
3. By being foolish

If you ever want a peek into the world of online poker and hear the stories of players going all-in, both in the game and the industry until it crashed and then reopened, then check out *Bet Raise Fold,* a successful Kickstarter movie by Jay Rosenkrantz. Poker professional Tony Dunst has a great line in that film; he says:

> *You try to make the best choice you can, and then leave what's left to destiny and each day has a little bit of mystery going into it.*

Going all-in is a powerful way to live life, but it must be done the right way. So from the start, let's delete the third way of doing things, foolishly, from our list. We'd never encourage a person with no skills, talents, connections, or Action Cards to go all-in. That would be both irresponsible and reckless. Little wonder, then, that Simcha's favorite quote from his mentor is:

> *When you invest in your business you make some money, but when you invest in yourself, you make a fortune.*

That leaves us with two options we can reference: people who have invested in themselves and people who know a winning hand from a losing hand.

## It's All about Trust

Yes, the all-in approach is a trust system. You trust that you'll succeed in the next step. You trust that the next move will work for you, whether by holding a winning hand or executing an awesome bluff. You put trust in the power of your next move. After all, it's not the last hour of your life, so there are likely more moves waiting for you in the future.

Now, how do you know whom to trust?

It's a common assumption that people can avoid going all-in and in that way, avoid all risk. What most people don't realize is that they are *already* all-in, all the time.

It's amazing how many people wrongly associate going all-in with foolishness or recklessness, and it's sad how many people don't trust themselves because they view themselves in that third category. They don't realize that they are smart enough to make good decisions or that they can leverage the world's knowledge on the Internet to help them make great decisions. They haven't yet realized that not trusting themselves comes with a huge price tag.

Allow us to raise those glorious stage curtains of your life and show you that you are already all-in, and have been for years, but have been playing blindly in systems that are collapsing.

## You Are Already All-in

Yes, you read that right! You *are* already all-in and have been for most of your life. But many people, are all-in in the wrong way and in the wrong areas, by default, having been born and raised to think according to systems that are collapsing and based on the wrong values, which are becoming increasingly outdated by the day. Unfortunately, too many people still view upholding these systems as demonstrating responsible behavior because it's what others do, and have been doing for decades and more.

So let's look into the mirror, turn on our strongest lighting, and take a closer look.

Here are the areas of your life where you're already all-in: banking and economics, education, health, real estate, and more.

### You Go All-in Financially

. . . when you invest your money in banks. You trust that the bank will be there tomorrow and so will your money. You trust that the bank will allow you to withdraw the money you put in, and others trust that when you write them a piece of paper called a check, it will be honored. But what if the banks collapsed tomorrow? People don't often think about putting all their trust into a system that could be gone tomorrow: "That can't happen; it's a bank!" Right? But here's what happened in 2013.

The headlines in March 2013 described how banks in Cyprus froze depositors' money until it was determined how much it would take to prevent the government from going bankrupt. In October of the same year, customers whose accounts held over €100,000 lost almost 50 percent of their money. It was automatically turned into stock shares for them in a collapsing system. Basically, people were forced into becoming partners with the same failing entity that seized their money in the first place. But Cyprus offered a cherry to top off their crème-de-la-crème action. According to the *law of citizenship by investment*, if you had €3 million or more taken from you—and some did—you officially became a citizen of Cyprus. Yay!

Would you be thrilled if the same bully who beat you up and stole your lunch money offered you a partnership on *some* of that money, but at a cost? People were financially decimated because they went all-in with the banks. Fiction is never as crazy as real life can be!

## You Go All-in with Your Boss

. . . spending every workday and maybe even some overtime over the course of a month, giving your job and boss your time and energy. You trust that at the end of that month you'll receive a paycheck that should translate into money as compensation. You expect that paycheck, and you expect to be able to cash it.

But if for some reason your paycheck never comes, or it does but it bounces, then you've literally lost out on a full month of productive time. What a massive opportunity cost! Yet we blindly buy in and trust some company to pay us, and on time, too! There isn't more all-in than that. You'll never get your month back if your boss, nonprofit, or company doesn't pay you.

## You Go All-in with Your Business

. . . when you provide your customers with a product or service that is paid for by check or credit card, trusting that the money to honor the payment system will be there. Basically you've invested trust and time into creating something for people to purchase through a system that you wholeheartedly trust. This doesn't even take into account the fact that you go all-in with your own business, infusing countless hours and labors of love on aiming for success . . . whether you end up actually being successful or not.

## You Go All-in as a Pedestrian

. . . when we step out to cross the road and trust that random strangers driving random cars will stop for us. We trust they know the rules, are paying attention, and are responsible drivers, but in fact we've never met them! When driving, we trust that the cars driven by strangers around us will stay in their narrow lanes, stop at red lights, brake in plenty of time to avoid colliding into other cars or people, and if they do collide with us, that they will stop, they are legally insured, they will exchange details, and that their insurance will pay for damages. We are all-in when it comes to trusting millions of strangers driving metal machines at every speed, and yet we don't even think twice about how all-in our lives are when we commute.

## You Go All-in with Your Relationships

. . . when you trust that spending time and effort socially is well invested. You assume, which is a form of trust, that when you need someone in your community to come through with something for you, that person will, realizing how much you've invested in his or her emotional well-being.

## You Go All-in with Your Pension and Social (In)Security

. . . when you believe you'll collect an income after retirement and for the rest of your life based on investments that people you don't know are making for you. People go all-in, thinking their eyes are wide open when in fact they're trusting a really risky system. We're stunned to think about how many people feel sure that's the safest route, planning to rely solely on pension or Social Security payments. From the early 2000s, the sad truth was revealed about the actual frailty of 401(k)s in the United States. Millions of people had been assured that 401(k) pensions would secure their golden years. Brightly enticing, this antidote to old-age hardship not only eroded but almost completely dried up overnight.

As for the employee mentality, people go all-in when they forgo happiness for the sake of continuing in a job that brings them no pleasure, and which can actually be a toxic environment, because of the virtual carrot dangled before them that comforts them with the thought that they're *just* several years away from getting their pension and Social Security.

## You Go All-in with Your Health

. . . when you trust the systems around you to provide care with the most appropriate medicines, treatments, health practitioners, information, and coverage. So how is it that we keep going all-in, even though the largest pharmaceutical companies are continually being slapped with lawsuits for billions of dollars?

## You Go All-in with Education

. . . when you expect your children to reach adulthood with relevant knowledge all because you placed them into some school system. Look at the trajectory: kindergarten, 12 years of school, and several more for higher education. Young adults are so busy learning for later that many are not being and doing for now! Yet we continue going all-in by trusting the system to provide us the tools and skills needed for success. Interestingly, among kids and youth now, there is a growing realization that they can detach from these collapsing systems and glean whatever they need from online and offline communities and resources.

It's an increasingly popular path currently labeled *unschooling,* or, as described in a great TEDx Talk given by an amazing 13-year-old speaker, *hackschooling,* in which learning takes place through experiences, connecting with interesting communities, apprenticeships, and focusing on whatever the hackschooler would like to learn.

## How Responsible Are You?

Somehow we've been trained to believe that when you go all-in for *yourself,* that's a mark of an irresponsible attitude, but going all-in to current operating systems run by other people *is* somehow responsible.

## All out versus All-in

New Entrepreneurz focus on learning the right lessons from their life experiences. They don't go *all out* because going all-in failed them: That would be the wrong lesson. So what's the right lesson? Start going all-in but in the right places. Specifically, start going all-in for *you*!

## The Solution: Trust Yourself First

In our events and mentoring sessions, we see how nervous, doubtful, and conflicted participants become when the system they're thinking about trusting is themselves! People think twice, five times, and more. New Entrepreneurz don't fit this pattern. Their system starts with the opposite angle: *First, I'm going all-in with myself, and then I'll give due diligence to checking whether I want to be all-in with systems that others have put in place and are recommending.* "Look,"

New Entrepreneurz say to each other, "I don't know you yet, or whether you're going to want to win with me or help me win the game of life. But I know myself, and I know that I want to win, and better yet, would love to win with other New Entrepreneurz who want to win the game, too."

That's why they choose to be among the right communities and listen to the right information from the right people. That's what allows them to build a team of winners with whom they can play the game of life.

So all-in is about making the right choices. If you'd never considered yourself an all-in type of person, you now know you were wrong. You *are* an all-in type of person! Your all-in attitude has just been linked to the wrong areas of life, areas that don't serve you well.

The entrepreneurial all-in attitude requires trusting yourself first and foremost. It serves as the foundation for all entrepreneurship: Trust yourself with having what it takes to win the game. You may not have it all now, but with entrepreneurial thinking, you'll achieve what it takes to be a winner.

If you feel you can't go all-in for yourself, you're basically stating that you don't trust yourself and can't carry your own weight. Are you banking on a complete stranger to carry you where you want to go? But strangers will only take you where *they* think you should go, or worse, they won't take you anywhere!

This is the purest message of the FreshBiz game, its core, as we get people playing, winning, and developing their confidence in themselves, which they'll bring to the real world knowing that no matter what the challenges and obstacles, they have the entrepreneurial mind-set that will allow them to win with ease. The board game and digital game allow people to practice breakthroughs and winning, so they can take that practice and seamlessly continue it in life.

## Are You Ready to Be All-in for You?

When Ronen sold his house to print the first 1,000 games of FreshBiz, outsiders found it hard to accept that his move was perfectly reasonable. That's because many people never stop to explore deeply the idea that having a house with a mortgage is also a form of going all-in. But let's take that concept apart at the seams for a moment: Isn't it no more than going all-in for buying the *bank* a house and working very hard to pay all the interest so that in 20 or 30 years, the bank will be kind enough to let you have it back? What does a mortgage mean in actuality? It means you pay one-and-a-half to two times the house's current cost so that it can be yours 30 years down the road, and hopefully retain its original value or possibly increase in worth!

So people put a lot of trust in the banking system and the real estate market in the hope that later, having worked hard for days, months, and years, they'll realize their investment. If you can't make the payments or are late too many times, your partner, the bank, will quickly confiscate your home. You accept those terms, however, because you trust the bank and the market.

But take a look at the telling etymology of the word *mortgage*: from *mort* meaning death and *gage* meaning pledge. Is it any wonder there's a saying that goes, "I'll be paying back the bank until the day I die" or its variant version, "I owe my soul to the company store." Is that the kind of all-in that does it for you?

Ronen responded to people's comments by explaining the all-in mortgage concept and then indicating that he'd rather go all-in with believing in himself and his ability to turn the money from the sale of the house into a much better business investment for himself and his family . . . without having to wait a few decades to realize it!

As things came together stage by stage, Ronen demonstrated to the skeptics around him that receiving a prize in 25 years for putting his trust in the bank and real estate systems wasn't what interested him. Instead, he felt like he received a prize every single day for living his dreams and attaining creative expression through FreshBiz. The company's valuation climbed to far more than the house could have ever been worth 20 years later, and meanwhile, he was living the dream and going all-in for himself.

As Ronen summarizes: "It's not that either you go all-in, or you don't. You're already all-in. So it's about switching the all-in mind-set over to a different system. I went all-in with my business, vision, dreams, and skills and I thank God for the courage to do so because I knew I had a winner."

## Step 1: Play the Numbers Game

Let's say you want to buy a $500,000 house. You deposit a down payment of about 30 percent and take on the rest as a mortgage. The monthly payments tend to be around the same amount as monthly rent for the same house. Thirty percent is a sizeable $150,000. Let's say that $150,000 came to you from savings, your parents, or any other legal way. You now have two choices: One is to use it as a down payment for that house and lock in monthly payments for 30 years to live in the same location; the second is to go all-in for *you!*

Making that down payment on a house can be interpreted as indicating your belief that four walls will create more value for you than you yourself can over the next 30 years. That's why banks lend out far more as mortgage loans than as small-business loans. It's up to you to prove the banks wrong.

## Step 2: Invest in Yourself

If you're going all-in for you, that means getting effective education and learning through accelerated learning programs, promoting your business, experiencing transformational self-development courses, and more.

Do you think you can turn that $150,000 investment in yourself into $500,000 over the next 30 years? This year alone we will have done that with just one of our revenue streams: game sales. Producing $500,000 over the next 30 years amounts to earning about $1,400 a month. You can do that through creating a great smartnership, getting a better job or a raise, starting a business, growing a business, or any other creative option you can devise! When you play those three decades with a New Entrepreneurz mind-set, you'll realize multiple rewards on a multidimensional level.

Those rewards won't just be money but will also encompass experiences, people, memories, self-discovery, and growth. You'll be able to live a great life open to all that the world can offer rather than be shackled to a mortgage. No matter what life trajectory you're after, *go all-in* because you want to and you trust yourself!

"Turn yourself into someone that you're willing to go all-in for," Ronen advises.

## Let's End with a Little Music!

When Ninet Tayeb won Israel's version of *American Idol,* she had no idea what type of fame that was going to launch her into. (Learn more about Ninet in the Interviews section at the back of the book.) Her album went platinum in less than 24 hours from when it was released, her cover of the popular Gnarls Barkley song "Crazy" has more than a million views on YouTube, and she's shared the stage with many famous musicians and even puppets, but what makes her rock is her style!

Her pursuit of authenticity and choice to go all-in with making music on her terms rather than just be another musical product for consumption is why we were excited to interview her. She shared with Ronen that it took her a little time to trust her intuition and leave some of the celebrity noise behind so that she could really hone her amazing gift of music. But going all-in for her, rather than her record label, critics, and advisers, is the fire in her voice and performances that sets her apart from everyone else.

## Put Yourself at the Top of the Going All-in List

The one basic skill you need for enjoying the endless possibilities whether it be in music, business, or relationships is to trust that you have what it takes to find the right tools, people, and methodologies that will guide you to being successful in going all-in for you.

If you are planning on going all-in one day, then we ask: Why not today?

# 9 Teaser

## You've Already Won the Game

*We didn't lose the game; we just ran out of time.*

—Vince Lombardi

**Figure 9.1**    Yosef Adest

## You Are Going to Win the Game

Our favorite story to illustrate this point aptly is that of the businessman and the World Series.

A huge fan of baseball in general and his own city's team in particular, the businessman was elated that his team made it into the World Series. He couldn't wait to experience it! Suddenly he realized he wouldn't be able to watch it because of an overseas meeting in a country without technology. His wife was happy to record the World Series for him in his absence. He even made her promise not to spoil the surprise by telling him who won. Returning from 10 days away, he avoided checking his smartphone and didn't look up at any billboards or down at any papers. The businessman stayed lost in the music of his headphones until he got home, gave his wife a kiss, and ran inside to sit down in front of the TV. Just as the game was about to come on, the businessman's neighbor shouts through the open window, "Crazy game. I can't believe your team won in the end!"

Are you kidding? After all that? All the preparation and maneuvers to avoid finding out, and now, zero surprise value! Oh, well. Now he knows that his team wins, but he watches the game anyhow. In the first few innings, the opposing team hits home run after home run. The next few innings . . . they continue scoring runs! By the time the last inning comes, the businessman's team is down 8–0. But because he knows the outcome, there's no fear, frustration, or trepidation. No sweat or heart palpitations as there would be if he didn't know. But there's something more that the businessman now knows: With a score like that, he must be about to watch the most incredible victory ever. Then sure enough, home run after grand slam after home run, his team wins the game 10–8. Wow, an awesome victory and without having to go through the emotional roller coaster!

You are going to win the game, friends. That's right. You are going to win the game.

As you already know by now, this book is neither a manual nor a magic trick for becoming a successful entrepreneur. This book is more like a tour guide through the mind-set and arena where the New Entrepreneurz (or at least as we see them) spend most of their time and energy.

Feel free to take and implement from the book whatever makes sense to you, according to your life goals, ambitions, and resources. We shared with you our best concepts and practices on how we play the game, and we hope you use some of them to better your life and win your game.

So what does winning the game look like for you?

Remember: Life is a time-limited game. No matter what your achievements or results, you can't change that one parameter. Also, because no one else can play your part in this world better than you, there is only one thing left for you to do: Play your part as best as you can, before your time is up.

Let's face it: Life's way more complex than a set of tricks or formulas, there are countless ways to live it, and it wears many different shapes and forms. We often don't have a full perspective until a situation is well into the past. Only then are we able to track the impact of choices and decisions.

But because life doesn't come with an instruction booklet, how are we supposed to know what being a winner looks like?

Well, therein lies its beauty, as they say. We get to choose! The power of free choice is at its best when setting the goal of the game. Being a winner is being true to your destiny, to playing the role you came to play here on this planet. Finding that role can sometimes be a life journey of its own, but we believe that the more you look inside and the more you listen to your intuition, the closer you'll come to understanding it.

We also believe that the journey is a really fun part of the game, with its amazing mix of evolving, learning, reaching new insights, and expressing your unique voice in the world. We believe that each of us enters this world with enough energy and available resources to win the game. Stick to your goals and your values and you'll make it. To see what that looks like, even when others don't make it easy for us, here's a story about a website pirate!

## Never Come from Fear—Rescuing Our Domain Name from a Website Pirate

Early on we bought the website freshbiz-game.com. We weren't exactly in love with a hyphenated name, but freshbiz.com and freshbizgame.com were both somehow not available. Of course, we put ourselves on the virtual list to be updated if and when either of those websites became available. Meanwhile, we forgot about the whole thing and continued playing the game, affecting people around the globe with our workshops, and sharing the photos and stories of the journey.

Along the way, an acquaintance of an acquaintance of Simcha's heard about what we do and suggested he'd like to get involved by making some connections for us. Not crazy about his style of doing business, which surfaced between the lines of some of the things he said, nothing came of his conversation with one of our partners, which concluded by saying that we'd be in touch if something tangible and appropriate came up. We thought that that was the end of it. Wow, what a surprise when a couple months later, he sent us an e-mail saying that he'd purchased the website freshbizgame.com but would happily sell it to us for *only* a few thousand dollars! Wait . . . what?! To this day we still have no clue how we didn't get an alert when it became available, but somehow this guy did and dove for it.

We explained to him that we don't negotiate with terrorists! Nothing moved on either end for more than a year. Simcha had no idea it was one of his Facebook friends who'd tracked our success and bought the website out from under us—but once Simcha found out, on his thirty-fourth birthday, he took immediate action.

"Initially I was infuriated at the betrayal by someone in my *friends* network!" Simcha related. "To think that someone in my Facebook community would do that! I breathed deep, let the anger dissipate, and had a glass of wine before opening a line of communication through an e-mail to him. You see, when we play the game of FreshBiz, we assume integrity and that people are great, so having cooled off, I opted for that voice. My idea was to try and bring him up rather than be brought down."

"So I wrote him an e-mail," continued Simcha, "saying that since it's my birthday and since there's a baby on the way, I want to be complete with the people in my life. So I brought up this incident which I found very disconcerting. Explaining to him that especially because our purpose is to inspire Win-to-the-Winth-Power thinking and smartnerships, I was really let down by him. To me his action felt like he chose to take on the role of a pirate holding a valuable hostage for the sake of bullying us into a one-sided arrangement. My request was for him to be fair toward us, especially since we'd never research what he's busy with in order to buy out Web addresses from under him with the intent of selling them back to him for a profit. There was a pause during which I realized that this whole episode yet again demonstrated the truism of those famous words, 'Commonsense is not so common.'"

What shocked Simcha most was when this so-called friend communicated his original intent. He'd bought the domain name as a bargaining tool of value for partnering with us! But partnerships are created through bringing value to each other, not from stealing or kidnapping value from each other. When the power you bring is from something you stole rather than generated, it's tainted. Needless to say, this individual's e-mail back to Simcha was defensive and unapologetic, delineating his legal right to buy any website name he wants. That's when it became obvious that continued conversation was going to be futile.

"For the sake of considerateness and to feel that I truly gave it my all, I walked him through everything one more time," Simcha remembers. "I was truly committed to being self-expressed in my communication with him, and not attached to a specific result. The worst-case scenario was simple: (1) Nothing changes from how things were the day before (2) FreshBiz continues having a hyphen in the site name. I knew we'd still win the game, even if there was a minor inconvenience along the way."

"And that's the great lesson: *Never come from fear*. The FreshBiz team never comes from fear, and I wanted to emphasize that he cannot bully a person who isn't available to bully. So once again, I reiterated that I'd never do anything he'd perceive as harmful. The way I see it, he can either transfer us the domain name to redeem himself, sell it to us for the standard price, or do nothing and we'd all feel icky. That message closed by saying there'd be no more e-mails or calls from me, and that this was my last attempt."

Within 24 hours, the domain name was transferred to us, he didn't want our money, and freshbizgame.com finally became our website. The whole thing is similar to that story we're told as children, about the sun and the wind fighting over who is stronger. The wind blew hard, cold air, and the woman on the street just held on to her coat tighter and tighter, while the sun shone its warmth and brightness until the woman simply took her coat off.

When you don't come from fear, when you know what game you're playing, and when you know you'll win, you can truly take a path of least resistance.

By the way, even if this story hadn't had an all's well ending, we were set on communicating in a self-expressive manner, and we did. We declared early on that winning the game was an inherent element of that self-expression and not dependent on external results. Happily for us, the episode wound up being a double win.

## Another Day, Another Step Forward

Every day, move forward toward better self-expression. That's what winning the game is about. By this stage in the book, it's clear that the race for stuff, which others claimed to be important, is so far from the truth.

The stuff we want or really need should be viewed as prizes, not the goal. Growing, learning, evolving, and creating the space for others to do so is how we see winning the game. We can each choose to be better today than we were yesterday, to learn and gain new experiences, and then to use them to develop new insights that allow us to adjust and fine-tune the way we play.

To us, living that way means . . . you've already won the game!

## New Entrepreneur7

That's right; this time we spelled that word with a 7 at the end. That's because we're about to present you with the seven major concepts that we see as best defining how New Entrepreneurz play and win their game.

Here they are, and here's how New Entrepreneur7 use them!

## 1. Belief

New Entrepreneurz know they can win their game. That's why they don't need or ask for anyone's approval. Just imagine you're standing in a coliseum with thousands of cheering spectators watching. In front of you is . . . a pea! Every type of contraption, from an old pitchfork to the latest smart gadget on Kickstarter, is arrayed on the ground, ready and at your disposal.

Your mission is simple: Pick up the pea. You have 12 hours in which to do it.

Would you find that challenging? Would you be nervous? Even if you've never been in that exact scenario before, you already know how quickly you'd win that game! Entrepreneurs look at turning ideas into reality with that type of no-problem approach because they have abundant resources at their fingertips. Their approach follows a simple equation:

$$\text{Mind-Set} + \text{Tools} = \text{Success}$$

Therefore, any action appears as possible and as easy as lifting a pea.

## 2. Activators

New Entrepreneurz function along a simple axis: "If it is to be, it's up to me." They're proud and excited to take responsibility for their proactivity. Choosing proactivity in their being, doing, having, and creating, generates real power. They are driven to make things happen through activity and aren't just waiting for something to happen to them. Some actions will lead to direct results, whereas others will need more time to actualize. Either way there's forward movement along their trajectory.

## 3. Storytellers

New Entrepreneurz are storytellers who use their lives as the manuscript in which they record their journey. Also, because they love the journey, they generously share it with the world. Entrepreneurs don't wait for the exit to be happy. That would be like waiting for the fairy tale to end with "And they lived happily ever after" before starting to enjoy the story! Because they understand that the journey is the reward, they experience it as a kaleidoscope of experiences to share around the campfire.

## 4. Collaborators

Knowing that they can win, and win faster with others, New Entrepreneurz always seek collaboration. Sharing platforms, creating joint ventures and smartnerships, and opting to expand the pie for everyone makes each action reverberate with power. New Entrepreneurz understand that they can win the game without beating someone else down to do so. The competition they face is between who they are and who they could be. Because they're competing with themselves against time, they don't waste time competing with others. Collaboration is an approach that lets them and others expand life experiences like never before by focusing on bringing value to all.

## 5. Seeders

New Entrepreneurz believe that everything is a seed being planted. The seeds of relationships, education, love, and more are being scattered around the world by the millions. Some will sprout immediately, whereas for others, it might take years. New Entrepreneurz understand that to be considered a happy, successful farmer, only a small percentage of those seeds need to grow into healthy plants. Instead of worrying, they set possibilities everywhere as they test which combination of soil, sun, and water produce the best results together.

## 6. Value Providers

Value to you and the world through products, services, and attitude is what the New Entrepreneurz really care about. They aren't looking to sell you something, convince you of something, or win an argument. Their approach is simple: If you're not looking for what they can provide, then you aren't their market, and that's fine. If you *are* looking for what they can provide, *bingo!*

## 7. Gamers

Life has never been a richer, more abundant game to play, and New Entrepreneurz love to play it. Understanding that the journey is the reward, they want it to be fun, be a source of memories, and some good laughs along the way—as children do when they play games. Yes, as kids we learned, explored, and discovered what works and what doesn't through the process of playing games and playing as a team. Why would we stop that now? The mind-set is one of serious playfulness. Sure, it sounds like a paradox to others, but to New Entrepreneurz it translates into playing the game seriously while having lots of fun along the way. The best part is that they can play as many games as they want, sequentially or simultaneously, and choose people from all over the world to play on their team!

## Look for the Magic

So next time you see something miraculous happening in the world of start-ups, entrepreneurial thinking, or just regular life, look for the mechanics behind it. Do you see the seven tricks of entrepreneurs in use? Maybe you'll find a new trick that's just been shared or created. Don't be satisfied with only reading about these tricks. Be them, use them, and enjoy the magic they create!

## Winning Isn't an End

It's not a happily ever after, either. Winning is the journey of doing what you love, loving what you do, and playing the game that you know you're meant to be playing. Winning is taking whatever you're given and applying that energy toward learning, improving, and moving forward. Yes, it may appear at times that we've taken more steps back than forward, but if we gain even a little bit of growth and development from those experiences, then in actuality we've been moving forward the whole time!

In the game of FreshBiz, as with the game of life, you have to throw the dice to advance. Forward, and forward again, we advance toward our goal. It doesn't matter if you roll a 1, 3, or 6. Knowing that you're going to be a winner lets you enjoy every dice roll because of the new experiences it brings.

Know what game you're playing, so you know how to win. That will keep you motivated and passionately excited as you play. Your wished-for lifestyle can be gratified to a very high level without it tipping the scales of excess. Fill it with meaning and your lifestyle will be a journey of fun moments with great people and experiences.

## Look for Quantum Leaps and Then Leap!

Let's try and keep things simple. In quantum physics, particles tend to disappear and reappear in various nonlinear locations. They do this with no traceable path and with no effort, unlike the physics of large-scale matter, which requires energy and a specific path to move an object from one place to another. Actually, the quantum particles are said to be making quantum leaps in time and space as they effortlessly move through different dimensions.

These same principles can be applied in creating quantum leaps in our own life dimensions that allow us to win the game easier than we ever could have imagined. First, you must feel certain that it's absolutely possible. Then, once you do, you can look for unlimited ways to leap. In the game of FreshBiz, this takes the form of a player jumping across the board much farther than they could ever go through the linear process of rolling the dice. Creating quantum leaps is a mind-set and set of skills that will help you win faster!

For now we just want to share a story.

Everyone's familiar with Sir Richard Branson: serial entrepreneur and founder and chief executive officer of Virgin, which deals in airlines, banks, music, and more. Aside from being an accomplished billionaire, he's also a great person, an incredible team leader, and a role model and speaker who advocates for change in the way people play business.

Knowing what he stands for and what his mission is about, we always felt he'd be a great partner for amplifying the FreshBiz message globally. As part of our 2014 business game plan, we planned a quantum leap around Branson playing the FreshBiz game. Without knowing the hows, details, or moving parts, we knew only one thing for sure: There is no way to plan a linear path for getting to him. So let's look for the quantum leap!

Because we know the power of crowdsourcing, just like we mentioned earlier, we tend to share our dreams and aspirations with our communities. In the same way that we're happy to try to connect the right people to each other, we figured that at some point we'd come across someone who could connect the dots for us. So we started sharing that we were looking for a quality connection to Branson. We shared it online with our community and offline at workshops that we ran in the United Kingdom or when we ran into one of his partners from plan B, Shari Arison, at a Tel Aviv movie theater. We continued throwing the dice, doing all our regular activities, all the while looking for our in.

It was when we were flown to Madrid to meet with our local business center and do some training that we were introduced to Santiago as someone who'd played the game of FreshBiz a few times and who was excited to play an active role in opening up new doors for FreshBiz in Asia. We had a great meeting and really enjoyed hearing Santi's travel stories. At some point we noticed that the magazine he was holding had a page featuring an interview with—you guessed it—Branson.

Of course, we popped the question: "Do you happen to know someone who can connect us with Sir Richard?" For the first time, we got a yes! Apparently, Santi had worked with him some years back in the music industry. Better yet, he pulled out his smartphone and showed us Branson's numbers in his contact list!

Boy, were we excited when Santi took on the personal mission of getting the FreshBiz game to him. We realized a special approach would be needed, one that would be unique and make us stand out in a positive way. Santi came up with the perfect idea. Richard has an island and the FreshBiz game has an island. Because he chose to make Necker Island his permanent home, we decided that he deserved his own special board game. Within 30 days, we manufactured six special FreshBiz board games for Richard and his team, where we replaced the FreshBiz Island (where the winner lot is located) with a real image of Necker Island instead. We even topped it all off with a personal message on each board as well!

True to his word, Santi flew to London to deliver the games personally as a gift to the Virgin Team. For us, Santi's trip, made just two weeks before this chapter was written, is already a big win, a great story to tell others, and an awesome quantum leap. We have no idea what might happen next in this adventure with Branson, but even if there is no next, "The journey is the reward," as Steve Jobs of Apple said so succinctly. Follow our blog for updates—by the time you read this book, you'll know if the story ends here, or maybe you will see cool pictures of Branson and us having a fun time playing the game of FreshBiz on the beach of Necker Island!

## It Isn't That Everyone *Is* a Winner; It's That Everyone *Can* Be a Winner!

This is life, the ultimate time-based game where we compete only with the clock and ourselves. That's it. There are many ways to win, and as long as you know that, and you know that you *are* going to win, then you are set.

You are going to win the game, friend, so have fun and enjoy the show!

# 10 Solving the World's Greatest Problem

*The way to get started is to quit talking and begin doing.*

—Walt Disney

**Figure 10.1**　Liron Smadja

We believe that the New Entrepreneurz have the opportunity and the responsibility to solve the world's greatest problem.

As we look around us, we can see many things that are not yet right in how the current game of life is played, and we presented many of them in this book.

From poverty to hunger, from draining our planet's resources to war and hate, humanity is facing many challenges. When we zoom out and take a wider look, it's easy to see that all these seemingly different aspects are merely symptoms of the same problem.

## The World's Greatest Problem

All that is wrong and unhealthy in the world can be traced back to one place, and that is the *mind-set* that we hold, or more precisely, the *wrong mind-set*.

After all, hunger in the world is not caused by a lack of food but by the lack of goodwill demonstrated by those controlling the game to share their people's abundance with those in dire need.

Poverty is not caused by the lack of money or resources; there is no shortage there, but by the injustice in the way the system was set up and then abused. Not to mention all the bureaucracy which makes navigating through it very difficult.

Greed, fear, abuse, and competition are but a few of the common mind-sets that are manifest in the world because of powerful people with the old-island mind-set. This creates bad behaviors, which lead to unhealthy symptoms, which ultimately negatively shape our world.

We've seen time and time again, that upon being given a chance to make a positive impact, people will choose to do so. The problem is that many who want to make a positive impact are lacking substantial resources, and many who have the resources, such as governments and big corporations, are too invested in the old game to really do something.

## The New Entrepreneurz' Role

This is exactly where we, the New Entrepreneurz, fit into the picture. As purpose-driven, game-changing, strong believers in self-expression combined with a Win-to-the-Winth-Power approach, it's up to us to make the difference.

Whether it's in the arts, businesses, relationships, or any other venture, remember that everything we do affects our mind-set and the mind-set of people around us.

We can choose to have the right effect on the planet.

Imagine a world where everything you do, every product you buy, every song you listen to, every show you watch, every book you read, or every game you play is a move forward toward solving the problem instead of enlarging the problem.

We can make those choices, now that we know the impact they have on our lives. We can choose better instead of more, and we have the power and responsibility to inspire others to do the same.

As New Entrepreneurz you can now shape your business and life to make a positive impact and present your customers and communities with better choices.

Just as 2 Degrees Food does with its health bars, 52Frames does with its photographers, or GameChangers 500 does with its achievers, we can each play our unique role in solving the problem.

None of us needs to solve the entire problem for everyone, but we can join forces in making a huge difference.

## One Game at a Time

At FreshBiz, we choose to solve the world's greatest problem one game at a time. Each time someone plays the FreshBiz game, he or she is rewiring his or her brain to a mind-set that is more collaborative, open, creative, and daring. This creates a long-lasting and real effect across the many dimensions of life.

Yes, it is *just* a game, but isn't everything?

We challenge you to start changing the games we play across the spectrum, the way Sir Ken Robinson has taken on education, Phillip McKenzie has taken on influencers, Ninet Tayeb has taken on music, or Hickies has taken on fashion.

The New Entrepreneurz are the game changers who can be found playing different games across the spectrum. They are the business owners, the managers, the lawyers, the moms and dads, the lovers, the educators, the artists, and the healers.

Entrepreneurship is no longer just about business; it is the new mind-set.

As Pink Floyd sang, "Shine on, you crazy diamond!" We look forward to celebrating with you on the New Island! Welcome to the tribe.

# INTERVIEWS

## Ninet Tayeb, Singer-Songwriter

As we first started writing this book, we knew that we would love to feature in it some of the people whom we came across and whom we saw as great examples of the manifestation of the spirit of the New Entrepreneurz.

Entrepreneurship is a mind-set, it's not a job description, and it can be found all across the spectrum. A great example of it is presented in the work and spirit of Ninet Tayeb.

Ninet is an Israeli artist, a singer-songwriter, and a great performer with a unique story. At age 20 she launched into the music scene as the winner of Israel's version of *American Idol* in 2003. She became an overnight success and went platinum almost immediately, acting in movies and TV shows and launching an international career.

We chose Ninet to be featured in this book because of her choices and actions over the past 10 years. Her journey includes all the different elements of entrepreneurial thinking: leveraging opportunities, using her Action Cards, building a smart business, and really being all-in! What we like most about her story is her ability to keep true to her unique voice and message in a world full of fast money temptations and big success.

So here goes:

Question: How did it all start?

Answer: Ever since I can remember, I knew I was going to be a singer. I really saw no other option for me to be anything else but a singer-songwriter. It started by running shows for and with my dolls, using a fake microphone, to later in being the main singer in all sorts of plays, events, and songs. From early on I focused like a laser beam on this very strong inner calling I felt.

Question: What happened once you got on the talent show?

Answer: Since it was the first ever music talent show in Israel, no one really knew what to expect, neither the participants nor the production members. And right after the first few shows, we all realized that things were going to get crazy. It got to a place where I couldn't walk the streets anymore, and literally lost all privacy, and got even crazier when I won first place in the final show. Keep in mind, I was only 20 years old, had just finished my army service, and was still living with my parents, when all this success started rushing in.

Question: At 20 years old, starting right at the top, experiencing such high a level of success can be dangerous. How did you manage to keep your head straight?

Answer: Well for starters, it has an awful lot to do with the way I was brought up at home. We had the understanding that we all need to treat each other with love and respect and that each of us has our own part to play, whether it's onstage or offstage. I had a deep understanding that my journey is just simply what I am meant to be doing here.

Question: What was the biggest challenge you had to face that came with the huge success?

Answer: The main thing was trying to deal with all the different voices people were shouting around me. Each one trying to pull me in a different creative direction, like they all knew what was going to be the best thing for me. It was early on, and I remember feeling surrounded by a big circle of industry experts all trying to spin me in different directions.

Question: How did you deal with this?

Answer: I always had a very strong inner voice, guiding me. The challenge was to be able to get back to it every once in a while and not let myself get carried away by other people's choices for me. And, of course, it took me time to develop the trust and confidence in myself to confront all the experts, and everything was happening so fast. But I held on to my truth.

Question: Your first record was a huge success and it was produced by one of Israel's top artists. How did it feel to you?

Answer: Well, as a songwriter, I did get to work with one of my childhood idols as a producer, and the album hit platinum in less than 24 hours. For everyone else, it seemed like a huge success, but for me, I knew I was offtrack. I felt that I wasn't sharing my true voice, and recording it felt like going to work, instead of making art.

Question: So success is not about how many records you sell?

Answer: No! I remember being on the album tour, feeling that something just isn't right. I knew that I shouldn't be feeling the way I was when I was onstage and that this wasn't my dream come true even if other people thought it was. It was hard for me to share this with people, because it's like, "How can I dare have the chutzpa to 'complain' about not being satisfied when my record went platinum and my tour was completely sold out?" People around me just couldn't get it, but I got it.

Question: It's quite a brave move to do at 24, where you could squeeze that lemon of success way more, make great money, and keep the party going; why did you do it?

Answer: As I saw it, my only choice was to find my true voice. I had to understand if I have something to say and to find the way to say it, and until I find it, I can't keep doing things that are not aligned with my truth. I didn't care about the success or the money since this wasn't the way I was measuring it. And this is where my journey began.

Question: Can you share the process of this journey?

Answer: I started by listening to Jeff Buckley albums. He had a huge impact on my music and art, and it inspired me to go and learn guitar professionally at the age of 24. That was a new milestone for me in expressing my whole self in my music and it took me down a crazy path of exploration. I definitely found myself experiencing some dark days and challenges, in the pursuit of finding my way.

Question: What were your major insights from that process?

Answer: That I wanted to focus on my voice as an artist and not on the peripheral stuff like publicity and paparazzi. I learned that I have a lot to learn about music, songwriting, performing, and self-expression. But most important, I understood that I have a unique voice to carry, I have things I want to say, and that is the most important thing of all.

Question: What do you see as the next step for you?

Answer: For now, I focus on being more and more precise with the message and being able to express myself at a higher level. I don't regret anything I went through, since now I have the understanding that every step along the way was the right move at the moment, as painful as it might have been. It happened so that I could get to exactly where I needed to be.

Question: If you don't measure success by album sales, how do you know that it's working, that there is a progress in the right direction?

Answer: I know by the reaction of the people who attend the shows. Lately I get more and more feedback and I listen to it . . . to the impact that the show had on people and I can see the deep way that people shift.

Question: What advice can you share with our readers regarding success?

Answer: My best advice is to keep listening to your own authentic voice. There is a tendency to try and be like other people you see around you as role models. Well, learn what you can from them, but keep being true to yourself; express yourself and your message. I would say in one sentence: Create your own layers on top of everything you see around you that influences you.

Question: Where do you look for answers?

Answer: I observe. I look in both the inside and the outside and I can spend hours observing the world around me, focusing on listening more than talking. The best answers come when I am in an observing mode.

Question: What message do you want to send to your future kids?

Answer: Accept the differences and be patient with others who are different than you.

Question: What game are you playing, and what does winning look like for you?

Answer: I'm playing a game of making a musical difference in people's lives. I want them to be able to take a deeper look and be true to themselves. Winning looks like more people taking action to spread their calling, after hearing one of my songs or coming to a show.

## Iris Zohar, 9 Rooms

Schooled in New York, Iris grew up in Tel Aviv, where she studied economics, design, and feng shui. Working her way up from the bottom, Iris served as an account executive, a supervisor, and a vice president in some leading companies. After years of being an employee, Iris brought her seasoned taste of the world's finest into starting her own business. She established a very one-of-a-kind boutique women's club on the port of Old Jaffa in a charming antique home.

Mixing lifestyle, content, and fun, Iris created 9 Rooms, a perfect example of a smart business. She serves hundreds of women and has a magazine with more than 50,000 readers who make up her tribe. Iris does small things in a great way, because as she believes, God is in the details. We chose to present Iris to you because we see her as an inspiration to other female entrepreneurs who want to turn their unique ideas into smart businesses.

So here goes:

Question: How did you get to start the 9 Rooms project?

Answer: In 2009 there was the global economic crisis. At the time I was running my *Premium Brands* consulting company, and I kept hearing complaints from my clients about the bad days that are arriving and what will be next. I never like thinking of myself as the victim, so I chose to take action. It became apparent to me that people needed to start boosting their businesses, so I decided to arrange a networking event for women. The initial idea was first of all to change the mood, have some fun, and then to generate change.

Question: With all the clients you had at that point, why did you choose to focus on women?

Answer: I had the understanding that if I wanted to make a real difference, then women would be the way to go. I especially focused on targeting women of influence so I could achieve the maximum impact at these events. It was important to me to choose the right women, those who can actually connect and engage, and I wanted them to pay for that participation so they'd be engaged.

Question: How did it go, and how did it turn into 9 Rooms?

Answer: It was a huge success, and it was fun to get the recognition that "If Iris is having an event, you better make sure to be there!" At first some people were suspicious and trying to figure out what the secret agenda was, but it became clear pretty quickly that these were simply events to help amazing women connect and grow.

The events were exhausting to put on, but I just couldn't resist all the women who told me how much of an impact these events were having on them, their businesses, and their family lives as well. So I built 9 Rooms as a home; so that in addition to the magazine and events, we had a place we could all come to for that 9 Rooms' spirit and vibe. I wanted it available for people whenever they needed it, not just on specific dates and times.

The day we came to this conclusion, the contractor came right on in and built the bar. I believe that if you know something is right, then you just gotta act on it. There's definitely no reason to keep on waiting!

Question: Why 9 Rooms?

Answer: The name comes from the *bagua* of feng shui. Those are the nine areas of life where when we find the right balance between them, we experience perfect harmony. They are family, fame, career, wealth, partnership, knowledge, helpful people, health, and creativity. I felt that those nine areas alongside the intimacy of the rooms would make a perfect name for our new home. Success comes from balance. Business success is not just about making more money or having more customers; it's about being able to enjoy your work while enjoying your family life, love life, health, and more. This is what I wanted for my ladies!

And pretty quickly it turned from a list of 100 women who attended our first event to a list of over 50,000 women who are now part of the events, club, and magazine. I still find myself shocked by those numbers and the speed of our growth. I'm just happy that I've had the pleasure to personally meet and engage with about 10,000 of these amazing ladies.

Question: How do you see entrepreneurship?

Answer: To me, an entrepreneur is someone who chooses to walk his or her own path. Entrepreneurs don't just wind up stuck in someone else's game; they create their own. It's not necessarily about business and money, but rather it's about living and creating life on your terms and the way you see it. My goal is to supply a supportive environment for every woman regardless of her occupation or status. I want to make them feel great with their lives so they can keep on doing whatever they chose to do in life and excel!

Question: What is your mission in 9 Rooms?

Answer: We believe that when you have your well-being and you feel good about yourself, then everything you do is just done in a better way. And women need this more than anyone else. Women are engaged in acts of service almost 90 percent of the time, whether it be with their families, clients, or team members. So the question is, Where do they get their charge so that they can keep doing what they do? Who can take care of them? Who can serve them for a while, so they can just sit back, relax, and feel fully taken care of?

We are that place. And we take the time and effort to think about what will make them happy, engaged, fulfilled, fun, and relaxed. This has a huge ripple effect on everything else they do in life. We see them blossom into better mothers, partners, businesswomen, lovers, and better people in general.

I see this as my personal mission.

Question: What is the business model of 9 Rooms, and how is that aligned with the concept?

Answer: We are a boutique women's club, and once the membership is paid, everything is included. So our space can be used to run business meetings, meet other women, attend special themed events, enjoy facials, chocolates, and coffee. We wanted to keep it easy and focused on value rather than pricing, which is why once you become a member, you get access to everything we offer.

Question: What type of content do you provide?

Answer: Our magazine has everything I think women would find interesting except for politics and illness. I keep those things out of my house, since they can get it outside anyways. I just want to keep positive and healthy vibes so I can give our women energy rather than drain them. We prefer deep conversations around lighter issues.

Question: As a colleague, friend, and business consultant, what are your insights regarding women and entrepreneurship?

Answer: I think women have more than what it takes to be successful entrepreneurs and businesswomen. Talented women have the power to change the world, but as I see it, too many of them are still afraid, stepping back, and hesitating from living to their true potential.

Question: What do you do about this?

Answer: Part of what I do is run courage workshops for our members; I encourage them to share their Action Cards, and use the club as a platform to present their businesses and skills, collaborate, and get feedback. I think women should actively look for such opportunities, and I see my role as just giving them a little push in the right direction, so they can take those courageous steps forward.

Question: What game are you playing, and what does winning look like for you?

Answer: My game is women empowerment. I want to provide them with the right environment so they can come in, charge up, and then go back out powerfully into their lives.

## Jon Levy, Influencers Dinner

This is someone who embodies the spirit of serious playfulness in everything he does. Spending years in the world of sales, management, and self-development, Jon now runs his own digital media company that works with companies on creative influencers programs for their products and services. Jon is even more famous, as written up by *Forbes* and the *New York Times,* for his Influencers Dinner, a special monthly dinner with a group of 10 to 15 influencers in fields across the spectrum.

We chose to interview Jon because he is an incredible New Entrepreneur doing a great job building an Action Card co-op with some of the most amazing influential people out there today. Living a great life in New York City, Jon does what he does not to pursue profits, but to pursue mission, connection, and quality.

So here goes:

Question: What is something funny that has happened to you recently?

Answer: When the *Times* and *Forbes* picked up the story of Influencers Dinner and word got out, one of my friends was asked if he knows "Jon Levy, your billionaire friend who runs secret influencer events." Now, I am not a billionaire; I'm also not a millionaire, but I do have a great standard of living and am enjoying the quality conversation and people of the Influencers Dinner community. It's just funny to see how we turn people into exaggerated personas.

Question: Why do you do what you do?

Answer: I was 28, at a Landmark Education seminar called Wisdom. It was all about fun, play, and ease. The program leader said something profound that completely changed my life. "There are two fundamental characteristics that determine the quality of your life: the people you surround yourself with and the conversations that you have with them. So if you want to really affect your life to any real degree, just examine what you are saying to the people around you, what they are saying back to you, and who those people are." I want to have an extraordinary life and really create an impact, so I made up my mind to surround myself with the best in every single industry and have great conversations with them. And to do it over dinner, too! It's not shocking that the people who are real influencers in their fields, tend to be really awesome people. I also get an immense amount of pleasure from bringing people together; it's just in my DNA. Influencers Dinner was born as a unique way to do that.

Question: So why a dinner, and what are some recipe tips?

Answer: I wanted the experience to take place by preparing and eating dinner together. There's something special when you prepare a meal for yourself and others. So we spend about an hour making dinner together, and during that time no one is allowed to talk about what they do professionally. We want people to meet in a more natural way without the ego, status, or other credentials that could get in the way of great conversations.

Different stations are set up throughout my kitchen, so people have comfortable spaces, and whereas I used to be there from the beginning, now I show up 30 minutes into it. I found that people would lock on to me if I was there from the get-go, rather than connecting with each other. This event isn't about me; I'm just providing the space for influencers to bond and connect, so my coming after everyone else works out really well.

We began all sorts of secret traditions that don't make it into the articles, and we've had some amazing delicious dinners and others where, let's just say that I've had to rely on the drinks! Either way, because of the people and conversations it always makes for an extraordinary dinner.

Question: What is the goal of Influencers Dinner?

Answer: You know, I'll share with you something that I don't really share with anyone: the purpose document of the event.

Here goes: "Influencers, there are those of us who have the ability to guide and influence the course of our culture. We do this across countless industries with our decisions, activities, creativity, investments, and perspectives. It is an honor and a privilege to have this level of influence, but it is also a great responsibility. For those who wield this level of influence, we have the responsibility to not only use it to benefit our community, but for the betterment of our society.

Influencers is a private and secret social gathering designed for exceptional people to enjoy each other's company through the preparation and sharing of a communal dinner. These guests will form deep and meaningful connections that will invariably improve the quality of their lives and over time positively impact the guests' communities and the world at large."

Question: Beautiful. How many dinners have you had along the way and what type of guests?

Answer: It's crazy, but I'm getting ready right now for my thirtieth dinner! We've had over 300 guests, and the list, of course, is a secret but we've had famous actors, business executives, TV producers, CEOs, and so on. It really ranges throughout the different industries. What I found is that it's often the ones who are really influential that most people haven't heard of, who I personally get the most excited about. I'm a bit of a geek, so having over one of the most influential people in the comic book industry of today, was thrilling. But so was having over one of the cast members from *Breaking Bad* and reenacting one of the scenes at the dinner table. But also getting to hang out with entrepreneurs and visionaries like MakerBot's creator, who revolutionized the world of 3D printing. These experiences are awesome and so are the incredible, unexpected friendships that come of it.

Question: What is Influencers, beyond the dinner?

Answer: It's also working with companies on their digital strategies, some product and Web design, all that stuff. But in real, nondigital life, I help companies develop their influencers program and do events for them in an interesting and completely unique way. I tell people all the time that there's a big difference between just reaching out to bloggers and getting them to blog about your product or service versus building relationships through quality conversations with the right people. Too often, companies spend money on promotions, which is so old school, rather than on investing in deep relationships. I work with companies to develop programs so that influencers can relate to the brand, love it. And when it's great they naturally want to talk about it and when it's not, they are actually disappointed and want to help you make it better.

Question: What game are you playing, and what does winning look like for you?

Answer: Creating the space for quality people to have quality conversations and winning looks like just making that happen. Of course, I've been getting offers for sponsorships and people who want to license it and monetize it, bring it to other cities, and all that good stuff. But here's the deal; the money could be nice, but these Influencers Dinners, each one is a special and completely unique experience. I still feel like I don't fully know what this is. I'm not willing to just label it early and call it something just so I can monetize it and I don't know if I ever will.

## Lauren Walters, 2 Degrees Food

Lauren Walters and Will Hauser cofounded 2 Degrees Food, a great company that makes a healthy, yummy snack bar and gives away one nutritious meal to hungry children for each health bar sold. One bar = one meal.

The one-for-one model is a great way to set up a smart business because it meets the mission by empowering its community to make a difference while buying a great product. We talk about multidimensional winning (aka Win to the Winth Power), and that's why we chose to interview Lauren. The company wins; at the same time, so do the customers, the children, the campuses and students across the United States that sell the products, and many more. 2 Degrees Food is the opportunity to make a healthy choice while adding the social entrepreneur aspect of making a difference through feeding the hungry children around the world.

So here goes:

Question: What inspired you to start 2 Degrees?

Answer: It started by looking at the world and then asking some simple questions. These were questions that I thought about when I was in Rwanda seeing severely malnourished children and yet knowing that there is so much food out there (in the world). How could this be and how could this happen? Even more locally, hunger in America has been getting worse instead of better, so I started to think if there was a way for ordinary consumers to help make a difference for these types of children on a regular basis.

Question: How does 2 Degrees work?

Answer: The idea behind 2 Degrees is that individual consumers can help other people while doing something good for themselves . . . on a regular basis. We work on the one-to-one model, so every time someone buys one of our healthy, nutritious snack bars, we donate a ready-made meal in countries like those in Africa, Haiti, or even in some parts of the United States. But we've always thought bigger even from the beginning, like: What would happen if any time you bought any food product whether it's milk, yogurt, granola, salad dressing, or snack bars you could trigger the donation of a meal somewhere else in the world where it would make a huge difference? This got us really excited. We envisioned the idea that there would be a brand (2 Degrees) that is identified with the idea that every time you purchase a food product you are helping others. So it's not just about bars; it's about a bigger idea that can change the food industry on an everyday basis.

Question: How did you choose the one-to-one model?

Answer: We believe that if you give everyday consumers a chance to help, they will. We saw that when you present people with two different options in the same category, where one of them also provides the opportunity to make a difference, people will choose the one that allows them to make that difference. We were inspired by companies like TOMS, which gives away a pair of shoes, for each pair sold, to someone who really needs it, and Warby Parker, which does the same thing with eyeglasses. At this point, Warby Parker is well on its way to donating almost a million pairs of eyeglasses to people in need, but these are occasional purchases: shoes and glasses. While this is great, nothing is more important than food, or food for undernourished kids. And the best part is that food is an everyday purchase, so every day you have an opportunity to help others, and with a snack bar, maybe even multiple times a day!

Question: How would you feel if other food companies decided to copy your model?

Answer: Gosh, that would be fantastic. It's funny because ordinarily I'm a pretty competitive person, but there are 200 million hungry kids in the world and therefore plenty of opportunities for companies of all sizes to adopt this model. If we could inspire other companies to do the same in the food industry, that would be simply fabulous.

Question: What advice do you have for other companies looking to inculcate the one-for-one approach in their business model?

Answer: It really comes down to reframing how we look at profits, margins, and what we consider to be a success. Some people insist that they need massive margins for a sustainable business, but maybe not. We believe that earning less by giving more attracts the right people and forms the right bond with customers. These are people who will go out of their way to purchase our products, because we offer them the ability to make a difference above and beyond just making a purchase.

We seek to make a connection between the buyer of the 2 Degrees bar and the person they are helping. We let the buyers choose where the meal that is triggered by their purchase will go. So if someone is especially interested in fighting hunger in the United States or India or in the refugee camps in Syria, the idea that you can use the leverage of your purchase of a 2 Degrees product to help a child in another place is really empowering. It's more impactful than just writing a check or trying to rally for big government to allocate more money for aid.

Question: We heard that you chose smart distribution channels. Tell us about that.

Answer: Currently, we're sold across 500 college campuses both through Barnes & Noble and directly through food service companies. The students themselves are great ambassadors and they have done two things: They do excellent local marketing since they understand their community better than anyone else, and two, they introduce us to food service companies on their campus. So we are in the process of working out a great way to gamify the marketing efforts of our students sharing the 2 Degrees message across the campuses.

We discovered that students care about causes but they don't write checks to charities. They wonder what they can do that will make a real difference beyond attending a rally, a protest, or a fundraising event. We let students make a direct impact as often as they'd like, so they think about their seven health bars they snacked on during the week, turning into seven nutritional meals being delivered across the world. It's amazing!

And our staff is really motivated by the fact that they are helping to feed kids. We have triggered the donation of 1.4 million meals since 2011, which we see as a drop in the bucket and just a first step. Our sales guy is someone in his 50s who spent his career selling regular bars. He chose to come out and work with us at 2 Degrees so he can channel all the skills that he has accumulated over the years, into a good cause.

Question: What game are you playing, and what does winning look like for you?

Answer: We provide nutritious meals to the world by making it easy for people to care and actually have an impact. Winning would be us expanding our line, as well as influencing other companies to adopt this model so we can deliver tens of millions of healthy meals where they need it most.

## Mariquel Waingarten, Hickies

Hickies is probably one of the coolest companies out there today. It came up with a simple and beautiful solution to a very common problem: shoelaces.

Fun fact: Hickies was the first project that Simcha ever backed upon discovering Kickstarter! Hickies needed $25,000, and in the end, it went on to raise close to $160,000, with more than 3,000 backers loving this new idea of replacing shoelaces with colorful, funky, designed silicon strips called Hickies. Get rid of ugly, pain-in-the-butt shoelaces, and give your shoes a smarter look with your unique expression of colors and combinations.

Mariquel's husband, Gaston Frydlewski, came up with this idea originally. Now the two of them together, with their new team, are turning this into a big reality across the world. We find Hickies and its founders to be a great example of the New Shared Economy and what is possible. From their crowdfunding campaign to the shared workspace in Williamsburg, New York, and even the fun messages they share with their community, we were excited for this interview at their headquarters.

So here goes:

Question: What would you say is the Hickies message as a company?

Answer: Our message is about having fun, spreading the love, and sharing the positivity.

Out tagline is, "Love your kicks," which is fun because it's got a double meaning. The basic level is to love your kicks, as in your shoes that you kick on and off, and the other is to love your inner kicks, which means your passions and desires. You know, the things in life that you get a kick out of!

Question: How did you come up with the idea of Hickies?

Answer: Gaston was truly frustrated with his shoelaces. He didn't like how they looked or worked. So 10 years ago he came up with the idea of trading them in for something more fun and stylish, and he went on the journey of making this into a reality.

When Gaston first came up with the idea, we were both living in Argentina at the time, and he was only 21 years old. He had approached several business-people as potential investors in this project, but he got rejected for being too young with not enough experience.

So Gaston put things on hold and went to find a job in investment banking, to get some experience and make some money in the business world. He spent five years in banking and later on gained some more experience in international business, which has been really help-ful. Later on, he used that experience and invested his time and money into the product, filing for patents, and many other items that were part of turning this business idea into a reality. It took a lot of persistence to see this through back then.

Question: You are running this company as a couple. How did this come to take place?

Answer: We knew each other for about eight years, and it was right after we started dating that he started showing me the sketches for the Hickies. I was very impressed, but at that point, too occupied with my studies to get involved with Gaston or the Hickies. Gaston on the other hand was persistent with me as much as he was with Hickies and for six years he kept calling me, sending flowers, asking me out, until I said yes, and we have been together ever since, as a couple and business partners!

Question: What is your experience and insights from running a business as a couple?

Answer: Our main motivation for pursuing the Hickies business was so that we could be together. So we both got into the relationship and the business knowing that this was the perfect combination of what we wanted to create. When we first started dating, I was the owner of a very successful boutique hotel in Argentina. It was great that it was a success, but we found ourselves too busy working, and not spending enough time together. We saw a joined business as an opportunity to challenge society's view on relationships and to combine business with pleasure.

We see the business as an adventure, so although there are sometimes challenges and more difficult days, we always tend to come back to the basic understanding that we started this business in order to have fun and be together. And we are! So that keeps things in the right perspective. While working together in the same business has its set of challenges, being separated has its own set of challenges, so we realized that it's just a matter of choosing which set of challenges you want to deal with. We chose together!

Question: What would you say were two of your smartest business decisions regarding meeting your purpose and your values?

Answer: One of them for sure was renting an office in Williamsburg, New York City. Coming from Argentina, we had to choose where wanted to be headquartered. We chose New York, since it's a fashion capital, and we see Hickies as a fashion brand, not just a gimmick, or a onetime hit. So coming to New York, and Brooklyn specifically, was an important and smart move.

The second decision was to fund our project through a Kickstarter campaign. You see, some of the people we had approached for investment or financing would, of course, try to tell us how we should run the business, where to sell, how to market, how to price, and so on. We saw this as an old-school approach, and didn't want to lose our creative freedom. For us, the new-school approach was to crowdfund on

Kickstarter, where the market itself gets to choose what products people like best, how to price it, and it gave us real validation. The feedback we got was great. We got new ideas on how to improve the product, and we got valuable information regarding people's favorite colors and packages so it allowed us to plan our inventory in a very smart fashion.

Question: What has been your biggest challenge?

Answer: The biggest challenge is to be able to keep up with the speed of our business growth. As of now, we are selling in 13 countries, with 10 people in the United States and two more in Europe. We are focusing on growing our online and offline sales, as well as coming up with some exciting, new products. The challenge is to balance the growth, with the endless ideas that we have, and with the requirements of the market.

Question: What are you looking for in business partners around the world?

Answer: We first of all look for people who get our brand and culture . . . people who can just plug right into the spirit of Hickies for the long term and those who are looking to just increase their sales by adding a complementary product with what they are already doing. We want our partners to be willing to invest in the brand and use their best judgments on choosing the right location and how to present it. It's more important to us to find tribe members than those just looking at the profit margins or quantities of sales.

Question: You have a great online presence, an engaged community, and you tell a great story. How do you make this happen?

Answer: Everything is done very precisely. We have a community manager that we meet with every month to plan for what to present, stories to share, deals we can offer, and what pictures to take. A lot of time is spent on how we can really engage our community to be involved and share their Hickies stories and pictures. Our art director is very talented, and she makes sure everything looks great. At the end of the day it's a lot of fun, collaborative work and we love our team. The idea is to present the product not as an alternative for shoelaces but as a fashion item that is part of a lifestyle.

Question: What advice can you share with our readers who might want to turn their ideas into reality?

Answer: I can definitely say that you should always follow your dreams, but keep an open mind about it. In other words, pursue them but don't confuse persistence with stubbornness. Listen to the market and the universe, and be open for change. Gaston has had many, and I mean many, ideas. Hickies was the one that never went away. It was persistent, so *we* were persistent!

Question: What game are you playing, and what does winning look like for you?

Answer: We are playing the game of fun and self-expression, and we hope people are inspired to play, too. I just came across a beautiful quote that says, "Winning is not everything; the will to win is," and I see our business the same way. Taking this journey, we are already winning; we already feel like we won the game, just by doing what we love . . . together!

## Phillip McKenzie, Influencer Conference

The first year of Influencer Conference, which is a culturally, ethnically, and ideologically diverse gathering of tastemakers in categories across the spectrum, was 2010. Phil McKenzie, creator of Influencer Conference, gathers influencers together to share their inspiration, ideas, and best practices. He is a deeply committed man who is about value-based living and sharing purpose with great people.

We chose to interview Phil because aside from being super likeable, his mission puts influencers together to generate the powerful conversations that inspire people to get to the New Island. Influencer Conference has had published authors, executives, entrepreneurs, and many other tastemakers sharing the new mind-set and elevating the conversation.

So here goes:

Question: What is the behind the scenes of your creating InfluencerCon?

Answer: Influencer Conference started when I was an equity trader at Goldman Sachs, and I just found myself not happy there even though on paper I should have been. So after six years there, I decided to leave and go do something else without knowing what that something else was going to be. All sorts of interesting and random occurrences transpired and I wound up creating a men's magazine called *Free Magazine*. This led me to working with different tastemakers and influencers, and it really shifted how I viewed things. It is traditionally thought that influencers and celebrities are the same thing, which they aren't. We viewed influencers as a culture of people who share the same values and we wanted them to connect so that they could change the world. We created the first conference back in 2010 in New York City as a way to connect with influencers globally.

Question: What are you looking to achieve?

Answer: My goal is to become a truly connected community. We need significant communication, and we want to hit the right core values. *Values* are what we all share and what motivates us all. We see trends around the world and are seeing that more and more, people's values are where they are choosing to invest their time and work.

I want to make communities stronger through connectivity, structure, and organization. Culture and race are not as important as values.

Question: How do you decide someone is qualified to join the event?

Answer: Quoting from a previous Supreme Court judge, "I know it when I see it." As one starts opening up and communicating, it becomes obvious, just like when you have the intuition that tells you that someone would be great for your organization. It's not about someone being from a specific field as much as that they are passionate about what they do. Because what they do is who they are, especially now that we've broken down the separation between *who I am* and *what I do*. This is how I want to live my life and grow my vision. Values are seen as soft skills. Trust, integrity, vulnerability are often thought of as weaknesses, but vulnerability is actually the bravest thing one can be. Asking for help is strength. We need to move toward a different way of doing business; it's time.

Question: I've heard you talk about mindfulness and the rise of feminine values. What are your thoughts on these two things?

Answer: They overlap. Leonard Shlain, who wrote a book about this idea, traces the history of Western values using parallels between when feminine values were respected and the time of the Renaissance. For example, female form, inspiration, intellectualism, collaboration, sharing, empathy, mindfulness . . . these are the values I really care about and this is what started our road.

John Gerzema wrote "How Feminine Values Will Save the World," and we see this as a major push in the right direction. We seek diversity in everything we do. Feminine values are universal. These are just labels. We've created these dichotomies when dichotomies don't really exist. But we are seeing the world now through an excellent framework of great values.

Question: What do influencers do or don't do differently from others?

Answer: Well, I think that their level of curiosity is different. By nature, influencers are very curious and willing to go out on a limb for it. It's one thing to be curious and another to do something about it. Influencers ask questions and then if there are no immediate answers they actively seek to solve those questions. They are driven to find answers, create answers, or connect with the right people who can create the right answers.

I like to call it intellectual nomadism, where they will travel wherever they need and connect with whomever they need for the sake of learning and knowing. We don't want people just living in silos; we want the intellectual nomads who go out and explore many things and are intellectually diverse . . . often the people we see on TED Talks.

Question: What game are you playing, and what does winning look like for you?

Answer: The game I am playing is that of being a good friend and family member. My parents sacrificed a lot for me to be here in the life that I've got. That's it. The way I see it, family and friendship equals living a great life. Just like the famous quote [by Jess C. Scott], "Friends are the family you choose." I have been blessed to meet some incredible people on this journey and I want to be that back to them.

Winning to me is being happy, and I am so fortunate to be on the current road I am on. I wouldn't have met a fraction of the people I now know had I stayed at Goldman Sachs. I feel more rich and fulfilled. I eat well, am well, and surround myself with friends and people who are winning in life, with great values. I want to see influencers in the fight. I really think we are faced with serious problems in this world, and I view this platform as one way to unite us all and get in the fight to present a different alternative.

## Yosef Adest, 52Frames

When Yosef picked up 10 years ago from the United States to go live in the StartupNation of Israel, he had no idea that he would be turning into a serial entrepreneur as well. A true entrepreneurial thinker who is great at turning ideas into reality, Yosef created his own video production company; turns the music notes in his head into beautiful, flowing piano pieces; and built the artist community known as 52Frames.

52Frames is a yearly game with a new theme each week for beginner and expert photographers to capture. Artists come to life with their work, family and friends are interested and inspired, and the community produces extraordinary photos that will blow you away. Yosef was someone great to interview because he understands Win to the Winth Power and the smart business, and is an Action Card factory in the artistic community of entrepreneurial thinkers.

So here goes:

Question: What is the background behind 52Frames?

Answer: After getting the pretty typical college education and earning my BA [bachelor of arts] in computer science, my creative nature discovered the world of videography. I formed my own video company and got really good at filming and editing and that's really where I began to exercise my creative voice, working on amazing projects. It was just when I wanted to start developing my camera and photos skills that I stumbled upon a project and a community where you take a picture a day for 365 days. What a cool idea! I lasted close to 200 consecutive days which was difficult to do, but took me through an amazing process. So I came up with an idea to make it more accessible and fun and that's 52Frames: a project that takes a committed group of artists through a series of themed challenges each week to produce an image with that subject in mind.

Question: Can you give us an example?

Answer: Sure. We've had weekly themes that are more technical like Shadows, Out of Focus, The Rule of Thirds, or Shot from Above to themes for the sake of fun and inspiration such as Outside Your Comfort Zone, Shapes, Trees, On the Job, and many more. What's amazing about this is it literally shapes the photographers' reality for the week and gives them an incredible game to play of capturing the inspirational. So for the week of Trees, our Framers shared about how they literally noticed every single tree and what was unique about it, or during the week of Shapes, the community was seeing the world not as it is but in shapes. It allows artists to experience life each week with a fresh, new perspective.

Question: How many people make up your community of Framers?

Answer: As of now, the community is 180 people strong, from over eight different countries. And it's a combination of amateurs and professionals alike who share the unwavering commitment of posting an image a week by Sunday night. It's a strong community, and we really help each other out, work toward getting over obstacles, and are just there for each other. I'd say that half of people's involvement is about life, while the other half is about photography. Keep in mind that many of these people would still have their cameras sitting on a shelf somewhere if not for this platform that activates them. It's the Framers who can deal with imperfection, growth, and keeping strong to their commitment that are the most successful. And it's amazing watching everyone grow, develop, and have something extraordinary to show for it!

Question: Where are these images shared, and how does it work?

Answer: By the time this book comes out, we will have our official 52Frames website, but for now, we've taken the free route of a Facebook group. Without any marketing at all—just posting albums each week—our community has expanded from 50 to a weekly reach of 30,000 via Facebook alone. Because competition can be an incredible motivator, the picture that gets the most votes from our committee gets chosen as the cover photo to represent each album. After that we have the top three photos that our community strives to achieve, and of course, the selection is based on photographic creativity and skill. Once our website is launched, we plan on gamifying the process even more, and offering the community new tools to really expand the project.

Question: What is life like for Framers outside of the virtual world?

Answer: We have weekly photo walks in different cities as an opportunity for the local photographers to meet, enjoy, and capture. Additionally, every couple of months we hold an event in different countries for our community members to exhibit their work. I got to tell you, if there is one expression that I hear time and time again, it is that this project is life changing! Every week, throughout Facebook, people wait to see the latest coolest images. It doesn't matter if you are an artist or not; it's just something that you want to check out. I just came back from a 52Frames exhibit that we had in London, and I don't think

I've ever been more inspired, proud, and moved. The responses of people flying in from all over to have this experience that the community put together, and the artists getting to see their photos blown up on the wall; man, it was amazing!

Question: What is your vision for this?

Answer: I'd like to see the project get bigger and better. Obviously, not just anyone gets accepted, but I'd like to see more and more talented people joining our community, multiplying, and getting thousands of submissions. Creating a tight yet open community is what I want. Monetization is separate. There are so many different ways to do it, and of course, many people have their thoughts and opinions about what I *should* be doing. What's most important to me is that it be done the right way, the smart way, and in a way that truly respects the project's integrity. I guess you'll find out what that looks like later on this year, but that's all I can say for now!

Question: What game are you playing, and what does winning look like for you?

Answer: To create a space in people's lives for them to access creativity in a very pure way, is the game I am playing. Through the vehicle of photography, I would like for everyone to put a camera to their eye and frame a real life moment. This is something everyone can tap into. And regarding winning . . . the present day is what winning looks like. Right now! I have an upcoming TEDx Talk that I was asked to give, which is a dream come true. And hearing how much the project means to people, watching the participation, seeing tremendous talent and growth, empowering artists . . . this is winning and it's so rewarding as well.

## David Hopkins, GameChangers 500

Dave Hopkins is an author, an engaging speaker, and someone rich in personal growth. It's no wonder that he was the first person that Andrew Hewitt, founder and creator of GameChangers 500 (GC500), chose to have on board before launching.

Fortune 500 is the old-island model of success based on money, power, company size, and so on. GC500 is the New-Island model of success based on multidimensional winning for people, the planet, customers, and communities. So it awards up to nine badges to organizations for achievements in areas such as Reinvent, Meet the Mission, Everybody Wins, and more.

We're proud of FreshBiz for making it on the GC500 list and not only leading the way here in the StartupNation of Israel but also in the Middle East and the world at large. Talking to Dave is genuine and refreshing, and he and the team represent what the New Island's business and life practices look like. Essentially, they are building a role model for New Entrepreneurz, and they do a great job of shining the spotlight in all the right places.

So here goes:

Question: You coauthored a book about social entrepreneurship. What's the message?

> Answer: Our book is called *The Tactics of Hope: How
> Social Entrepreneurs Are Changing Our World.* My
> coauthor introduced me to that term back in 2003,
> which was pretty early. I remember as a kid growing
> up surrounded by great family and lots of love. I knew
> that I wanted to be an international businessman
> when I grew up, but then here's what happened. Each
> morning my school bus would take us through the
> really bad section of town where there was graffiti,
> drugs, and hookers, and then later after graduating
> from a great college, I went to Africa to teach AIDS
> awareness and started seeing extreme poverty and
> health issues like never before. I began asking the
> question, "What caused this poverty at home and
> these issues in Africa?" Sadly, it seemed that all roads
> and answers pointed back to big business.
> I realized that I wanted to be a part of the solution
> and not the problem and it seemed that social
> entrepreneurship was the key. It was the way to bridge
> the divide and choose to do business the right way as
> part of the solution.

Question: We were so excited to qualify as one of the
GameChangers 500 companies. Tell us what it is like
actually working with Andrew and GC500?

> Answer: So Andrew Hewitt is the founder and my
> amazing partner that most people know from his

TEDx Talk about GameChangers 500. I'm their first full-time employee in charge of making it happen, and even though we're still a young company, we're at an inflection point right now. Over the next six months, our goal is to reach several million people from students to businesses, and inspire them to become GameChangers. We award companies with up to nine different badges in categories like Meet the Mission, WinWinWin, Planet Friendly, Reinvent, and more, to acknowledge those doing great things.

We love making connections and building bridges for others that make sense. Right now, we are experiencing a supply-and-demand challenge where there are more people looking for something larger to be connected to, which is purpose. And what's lacking is a supply of inspiration and meaningful actions and practices that they can follow: a road map to show them how to do it and a model on how to emulate it. Our goal is to give people the list but also the tools to get there.

Question: What are you looking to accomplish?

Answer: We are driving aspirations so that people understand this new model for business is essentially the new cool. There are two main things that we seek to accomplish: The first is to drive aspiration so that organizations desire to be a game changer and the second is to shine the spotlight on organizations and companies that are role models leading the way and sharing their best practices. It's a great way to learn from each other.

Question: You see things changing?

Answer: I love Bucky Fuller's quote, "You never change things by fighting the existing reality. To change something, build a new model that makes the existing one obsolete."

This is exactly what we are doing! In the not-too-distant future, things will shift so you would never dream of building a business if it's built on any form of exploitation. We are letting go of the old way things are, left over from the old Industrial Revolution model of take/make/waste. Back then it was about growth at all costs, with no consequences and short-term revenue gains. The profit-at-all-costs model is over, and we are creating the new barometer for people to do business.

Question: Tell us a little bit about the GC500 business model.

Answer: Sure. GC500 is free and is based upon merit alone, and of course, we choose that in order to maintain the integrity of the list. There could be thousands of companies that are considered GameChanger companies, but only the top 500 will qualify as the GameChanger 500 companies. We monetize the business by allowing invited companies to opt in to a host of services, events, bonuses, a featured profile which includes the story of the founder, badges achieved, best practices, and much more! Just this past week we were invited by Harvard to interview three amazing GameChanger companies about their best practices: Warby Parker, New Balance, and Life Is Good. It was amazing! We will be rolling out more features and benefits later in the year.

Question: What's your vision for the website?

Answer: I see all New Entrepreneurz going to our website and spending a few hours there doing research before starting their own ventures. It will provide access for taking a deep look into some of the coolest companies' methodologies, best practices, the stories, and why they do what they do.

Question: What self-development have you done and what does it do for you?

Answer: There's no greater investment that one can make more than knowing thyself. It's a constant journey. Just last week I began incorporating meditation into my day. Wow, I've done vision quests, traveling, Landmark Education, Dream University seminars for dream coaches, coaching students and workshops on careers and developments, and the more I do the more it feels like there is more to do.

The key is to always be connected to a sense of purpose that gives back to others. I think of it as personal development less for you and more for the world. You see, when doing it to be connected to a cause that is outside of yourself then it becomes . . . "Here is the need in the world that I want to address and I'm willing to do this self-development in service of that greater need." It becomes such a joyful experience of education.

Question: How do you embody serious playfulness?

Answer: We will be gamifying the entire GameChangers 500 process so that businesses can strive to have more and more badges and be featured more prominently based upon those successes. Making it fun and making it cool to go above and beyond and then recognizing those for doing so . . . I think that is pretty serious playfulness!

The master in the art of living is my role model on the path to enlightenment. And I won't say that I have it all figured out, because I don't. But I'm working on it and I know that I'm moving in the right direction.

Question: What game are you playing, and what does winning look like for you?

Answer: The game that we are playing is the game of ushering companies into the new world of purpose-driven GameChanger companies. Winning looks like every organization around the world is a GameChanger company striving to be better no many how many badges they currently have.

## Jon Vroman, the Front Row Foundation

A phenomenal human being, this guy even has a son named Tiger! Jon can be found sharing his powerful message of living life in the front row on college campuses across the United States. Out of the world of sales, leadership, coaching, and personal development, Jon created the Front

Row Foundation. It gives its recipients, many of whom have terminal illnesses, the front row experience of their lives.

Interviewing Jon is refreshing because of how in tune he is with who he is and what he does. He lives a purpose-driven life, building an engaged community of people who care not only about making dreams come true but also about "living life in the front row." Jon is a great example of how being in action, the right way, creates expansive results.

So here goes:

Question: Take us behind the scenes of creating the Front Row Foundation.

> Answer: Sure! There are a few aspects to it.
>
> One: I was at a truly life-changing Tony Robbins seminar where I was asked a self-discovery question about exploring my contribution to the world. My heart told me that it was lacking, and I realized that it was an important aspect of my life that I didn't feel awesome about. So I woke up and wanted to contribute in a big way.
>
> Two: Later that year on my birthday in 2005, I was at one of my favorite concerts, a Jason Mraz show. There I was sitting high up in some back row enjoying the music, when I started to notice the fans in the front row. It was a completely different energy! Jason was interacting with them and they were interacting with him and it was just magic, while I felt on the outside of everything. It was such a metaphor for life; you are either a spectator in the back or a participant in

the front. It had a profound effect on my psychology as I realized that I wanted to live life in the front row, from then on!

Three: My buddy Jamie invited me to do a double marathon in the fall of 2005 with only 16 weeks to prepare. I was truly scared and needed motivation. So I told everyone that we were doing it for charity and that got me fully committed and accountable. I've heard it said that what scares you the most brings you to life. Well, this brought me to life, and I really enjoy the ride and want it to last forever. I love experiences and magic moments with the amazing people in my life . . . so we created the Front Row Foundation as the charity to run for. By the way, we finished the marathon successfully, too!

Question: Tell us exactly what the Front Row Foundation does.

Answer: Our mission is to help individuals and families who are braving critical health challenges experience life in the front row. So we put them in the front row of the live event of their dreams, which range from sporting events to concerts and all other live events in between. We give families the opportunity to have a larger-than-life live experience with their loved one who is battling a life-threatening illness. And people are awesome. Their generosity allows us to keep creating these life-changing moments!

Question: How many events have you done and what were some highlights?

Answer: We've done about 65 events so far, and they were all my highlights. But to name a few, we have an amazing boy named Jack who, in two days, will be seeing the magic show of his dreams, and we had a gal a few months ago who sat in the front row at the taping of her favorite show, *The Big Bang Theory*. We had Sophie, a special four-year-old girl suffering from a brain tumor, who we took see Kelly Clarkson, her favorite singer. This went on to become the best day of this little girl's life. Kelly agreed to meet us all backstage afterward and even took pictures holding Sophie, with the family. I cannot tell you how much this moved me to tears . . . and she passed away a short time later. But we and her family will never forget that experience together.

You know, at first we thought it was going to be all about the recipient. Later we realized that when one person is battling, everyone is battling. It impacts the entire family tremendously; it's so hard for them sometimes. We come in and create an event, memories, and an awesome story for them, that they wouldn't have without us.

Question: How did you engage people to participate in the foundation?

Answer: We built it by going to our family and friends first. We kept it very grassroots and did local events. Our first one was a combination of comedians, beers, and beef, and with a few hundred people, we raised our first funds. These events are also where we found our first recipients. So everything kind of started within and then expanded out from there. We run local events and fundraisers, and our community is just awesome. We currently have around $50,000 a year that comes in through monthly donations—everything from $11 per month and up.

Question: That's how you got your people engaged, but how did you really activate them?

Answer: Got it. We got good at telling the story. Two different stories to be exact: the story of the charity and what living life in the front row is all about and then the story of the recipients, who they and their family are and what they are currently going through. Sharing both stories across all of our platforms . . . people really connected and they wanted to participate. We got really good at sharing both so that people got it. As a matter of fact, we were just on the *Today* show last week, which was really exciting. It's just like in the game of FreshBiz; you can miss out just by not seeing something or not asking . . . so we saw something and we asked . . . and they answered!

Question: What's your vision for the Front Row Foundation?

Answer: That at some point, at every single live event taking place in the world, there will be a Front Row recipient. I'd like it to be the cultural norm for musicians and athletes to specifically start asking about who is their front row that night. And our shorter-term and more actionable goal is for this to not just be about one day, or one event, but about a relationship where we can continue to impact them forever.

One of my team members came up with something great: "It's a forever thing." That's how we feel. It's not just a onetime wish answered. This is a forever thing. We celebrate anniversaries of their experience with their families and really blur the lines between wish granting and coaching in living life in the front row. I cannot stress enough that this a lifestyle and not just a onetime experience. We love and believe in family and just want to support them through everything they go through.

Question: Where can people go to get involved?

Answer: Join the conversation, participate, follow the stories we share, and get involved. It's all on our website at frontrowfoundation.org.

Question: What game are you playing, and what does winning look like for you?

Answer: The game I'm playing is one of self-discovery and then sharing with others. The game of learn and share. How much can I learn and how much can I share? Winning looks like the satisfaction of knowing that I used my God-given talents and gifts for good. It's a game I feel like I can win daily.

# ACKNOWLEDGMENTS

**W**ow! Writing this book has been an incredible journey. First we want to thank God, the Universe, or however you refer to It for the inspiration, clarity, and energy to carry the voice and put together the pieces.

We want to thank Brian, Christine, Lauren, and the rest of Wiley's team for noticing, reaching out to us, and guiding us. It was a privilege and a pleasure to work with such an established publisher in writing our first book. And to Avi Staiman and Seree Zohar from Humanities Translations for an incredible editing job and really "getting us."

To our amazing spouses, Anat and Rachel, for being two of the coolest women on the planet. Thank you for your unconditional love and support with all of our crazy ideas . . . even if it sometimes means selling the house. To our parents for their love, guidance, and active investment in our business. And to the new generation: our children, Noy and Agam Gafni, and Maor Gluck, for their childlike inspiration—this book is our humble contribution so that they may grow up in a fresh new world.

Thank you Josh Weiss, our third FreshBiz partner and close friend, who kept the company going and thriving while we were sometimes in "Bookland." His general role in the company is filled with wisdom, and his ability to focus on the day-to-day practical logistics, behind the scenes, and relationship building keep us grounded so we don't just fly away.

And to our investors and partners in the vision: Dalit, Tami, Carlos, Bettina, and Johanan—we truly appreciate your trust.

And we want to acknowledge our FreshBiz Experience Leaders who run FreshBiz activities around the globe: Revital, Karen, Daniel, Lorena, Amman, Girish, Flor, Becky, Shoshi, Inna, Daniella, Jose, and the tens of FreshBiz Facilitators who have early on stepped up to be the new voice as amazing New Entrepreneurz.

A big thanks to all the people and organizations who appear in this book because of who they are and what they do in the world.

Special thank you to all those who shared their Action Cards with us as we wrote the book: Rivka and Yumi for giving us their home upstate for a week of writing; Yosef and the entire artistic 52Frames community for sharing with us their images for our chapters; Uncle Willy for providing his home away from home as a creative space for late nights; our awesome Internpreneurs: Ethan, Kady, Nicoli, Monyka, Gabe, and Jessica for being innovative entrepreneurial thinking Millennials; and Tel Aviv, Madrid, Jerusalem, and New York City for providing such cool locations and atmospheres for us to write in.

Of course there are all the friends, family, and FreshBizers who are too many to list and name. You're playing the FreshBiz game, attending our workshops, and engaging with our content, making it possible for us to carry our voice in the world. Last, we would like to thank you, the reader, for reading this book and choosing to join us on this journey.

See you all on the New Island!

# INDEX

NOTE: Page references in *italics* refer to photos.

"access trumps ownership," 55, 136
Achievers, 36
action, taking. *See* Throw the Dice
Action Cards, 79–96, *80*
   collaborating with, 88–90
   for college, 92–93
   as currency, 82–83
   defined, xii, 81–82
   inception of, 12
   networking with, 85–86
   power of, 81–82, 83–85
   reasons why people don't share,
      91
   sharing *versus* bartering, 93–94
   Smartnership and, 130
   using, 90–91
   value of, 86–88, 94–96
   for work, 92
Adest, Yosef, 76, 90, 215–219
Airbnb, 58
All-In, 141–158, *142*
   authenticity and, 157
   being proactive, 143–144
   investment and, 145–146, 156–157
   mind-set of, 144–145
   readiness and, 154–155
   trust and, 146–154

Bachenheimer, Bruce, 32–35
bartering, sharing *versus,* 93–94
belief systems, awareness of, 101

*Bet Raise Fold* (movie), 145–146
body image, 52–53
Branson, Sir Richard, 41, 173–175
business, starting. *See* Smart Business

certification, need for, 103–104
challenges
   overcoming, 38–40, 132–133
   "scaling-up challenge" *versus* "scaling
      smart," 134–135, 140
change
   generating, 115
      (*See also* Smart Business)
   optional and mandatory actions for,
      100 (*See also* Green Titles and
      Red Titles)
   *See also* games
coaching, 111–112
collaboration
   Action Card co-op for, 88–90
   defined, xi, 10
   shared economy and, 55
   Smartnerships and, 127–131
   winning through, 169
Communitycation
   defined, xiii
   for Smart Business, 124–125
competition
   problem of, 10, 50
   reluctance to use Action Cards and,
      91, 95

competition (*continued*)
  Smart Business as alternative to,
      115–117
  Win to the Winth Power, 73–75
Cowper, William, 29
crowdsourcing, 57, 173
customers, as community members,
      124–125
Cyprus, financial problems of,
      147–148

debt
  home ownership and, 8–9, 13–14,
      106–107, 154–155
  problems of, 51–107–108
"Deliberate" (Bachenheimer),
      34–35
*Delivering Happiness* (Hsieh), 93
distribution channels, smart, 202–203
donations, through one-for-one model,
      126–127, 199–204
Dunst, Tony, 145

e-commerce, advent of, 21
economics. *See* New Shared Economy
entrepreneurship
  entrepreneurial thinking, x–xii
  game of business and, 9–10
  Lifestyle Entrepreneurs, 25–28
  Lone Workers, 21–25
  as mind-set, viii
      (*See also* New Entrepreneurz)
  risks of, 8
  summer jobs and, 110
Entrepreneurship Lab, Pace University,
      33–35
environment
  ecofocus, 54–57
  environmental problems, 53
European Union, economy of, 51

Facebook, 118
factory workers, history of, 19–20

fear
  courage workshops for (9 Rooms),
      193–194
  of losing, 10
  rejecting, 163–167
Ferris, Tim, 123
52Frames, 76, 214–219
Ford, Henry, 41
Fortune 500, 43
*4-Hour Work Week, The* (Ferris), 123
Free Magazine, 211
FreshBiz
  definitions, xii–xiii
  game-based seminars of, 49
  on GameChangers 500 (GC500) list,
      44
  Get to the Island game, viii–ix,
      68–69, 174
  inception of, 9–16, 154–155
  Share Game workshop, 125
  website name of, 163–167
  workshops by, 15, 32
Fresh (boutique branding agency),
      8–10
Front Row Foundation, 19, 224–229
Frydlewski, Gaston, 28, 204–210

Gafni, Anat, 8–9, 13, 90
Gafni, Ronen, *2*
  biographical information, 3–8
  early business of, 8–10
  FreshBiz started by, 10–16, 153–155
GameChangers 500 (GC500), 36,
      43–44, 219–224
games, 47–69, *48*, *61*
  Gamers, 29–35
  Get to the Island game, viii–ix,
      68–69, 175
  life as, 49–50
  for positive change, 54–57, 60, 64–65
  power of, 65–68
  problems of old-school thinking,
      51–53, 57–59
  problem solving with, 181

questions about, 59–60
  for success, 170–171
  Throw the Dice and, 60–64
Gandhi, Mohandas, 54
Gates, Bill, 137
Gerzema, John, 212
Get to the Island game
  concept of, viii–ix, 175
  experiencing, 68–69
  website for, 69
Global Thinkers, 35–37
Gluck, Rachel, 23–24, 77, 107
Gluck, Simcha
  Action Cards of, 90
  biographical information, 23–24,
    107
  FreshBiz role of, 15
  FreshBiz website name and, 164–167
  multidimensional winning by, 77–78
Google, 37
Great Depression, 20
Green Titles and Red Titles, 97–112, *98*
  avoiding choices with Red Titles,
    108–109
  defined, xiii, 99–101
  entrepreneurial summer jobs and,
    110
  flexibility and fluidity of, 101–108
  health and wellness as, 109–110
  inception of, 12
  mentoring and, 111–112
  questions to ask, 111

habits, changing, 65–68. *See also* games
"hackschooling," 152
Hauser, Will, 199
health
  Front Row Foundation and, 224–229
  as Green Titles and Red Titles,
    109–110
  importance of, 52
  trust and, 151
Hewitt, Andrew, 43–44, 219
Hickies, 28, 204–210

Hill, Napoleon, 119
home ownership, 8–9, 13–14,
    106–107, 154–155
Hopkins, David, 219–224
"How Feminine Values Will Save the
    World" (Gerzema), 212
Hsieh, Tony, 93

identity, of New Entrepreneurz, 30,
    41
income, passive, 25–27
India
  economy of, 52
  Institute of Technology Bombay, 16,
    134
Industrial Revolution, 19
influencers
  Actions Cards used by, 86–88
  approach by, 213–214
  Influencer Conference, 86, 210–214
  InfluencersCon, 86
  Influencers Dinner, 87, 194–199
  New Entrepreneurz as, 53, 86–88
information sharing, importance of,
    36
integrity, 164
Internet, advent of, 20
Internpreneur, defined, xiii
investment
  in business, 8–9, 13–15
  going "All-In" with, 145–146,
    156–157

Jacks, L. P., 134
Jobs, Steve, 175
Jordan, Chris, 52

Kickstarter, 57, 207–208
Kiyosaki, Robert, 25

lean business, building, 136–137
*Lean Startup, The* (Ries), 136

learning
  Action Cards for college students, 92–93
  college education as optional, 102–104
  education and trust, 151–152
  game-based, 49
  higher education and, 7–8
  school and, 3, 10
Levine, Uri, 37
Levy, Jon, 86–87, 194–199
Life Hackers, 29–35
lifestyle
  flexibility and, 101–108 (*See also* Green Titles and Red Titles)
  Lifestyle Entrepreneurs and, 25–28
  Smart Business and, 133–140
LinkedIn, 85–86
Liss, Alexandra, 57
Lone Workers, 21–25
Lyft, 58

mandatory actions. *See* Green Titles and Red Titles
McKenzie, Phillip, 86–87, 210
mentoring, 112
mind-set
entrepreneurship as, viii
changing, 76
  importance of, 144–145
  for problem solving, 179–180
mission
  communicating, 49, 122–124
  higher mission of Smart Business, 119–125
money
  financial trust and, 147–148
  historical use of, 83
  home ownership, 8–9, 13–14, 106–107, 154–155
  investing in business, 8–9, 12–16
  investment and going "All-In," 145–146, 156–157
  lack of, 82

nonmonetary currency
  (*See* Action Cards)
  passive income, 25–27
  payment systems and trust, 149
  problems of debt, 51, 107–108
  stock market, 5–6, 20
  windfalls, 107
  *See also* Action Cards; New Shared Economy
mortgages, 8, 14, 106, 154–157
motivation, sharing, 120
multidimensional thinking, 54–57, 75–79, 199–204
multitasking, 32–35
music industry, 58. *See also* Tayeb, Ninet

Napster, 58
networking
  Actions Cards used for, 86–88
  Influencer Conference, 86, 210–214
  InfluencersCon, 86
  Influencers Dinner, 86–87, 194–199
  LinkedIn for, 84
  New Entrepreneurz as influencers, 54, 86–88
  9 Rooms, 120–121, 189–194
New Entrepreneurz, *vii*, 19–45, *18, 30, 42*
  challenges of, 40–43
  defined, viii–x, viii–xiii, 19–20
  Freshbiz defintions, xii–xiii
  as game changers, 28
  Life Hackers and Gamers, 29–35
  Lifestyle Entrepreneurs and, 27–28
  Lone Workers *versus*, 21–22
  questions for, 46
  "rat race" history and, 19–21
  role of, 180–181
  self-expression and, 41–44
  seven tricks used by, 167–171

Social Gamers and Global Thinkers, 35–37

transformation and, x–xii

*See also* FreshBiz; games; influencers

New Shared Economy

defined, 54–57

for lean business, 136–137

problems of old economy, 49–50

9 Rooms, 120–121, 189–194

nonmonetary currency.
*See* Action Cards

One Couch at a Time (documentary), 57

one-for-one model, for donations, 126–127, 199–204

optional actions. *See* Green Titles and Red Titles

Pace University, 33–34

partnership. *See* Smartnership

passive income, 25–26

payment systems, trust and, 149

PayPal, 103

"pay with a tweet" concept, 86

pedestrians, trust by, 149–150

pensions, trust and, 150–151

personal development, 139–140

perspective. *See* Zoom Out

photography. *See* 52 Frames

physical health. *See* health

planning, creating opportunities for success, 171–174.
*See also* winning

"plastic surgery" (for debt), 108

potential, realizing, 174.
*See also* winning

preexit strategy, 121–122

Premium Brands, 189

proactivity, 143, 168

problem solving, 54, 177–181, *178*

Quantum Leap, defined, xii

Ramsey, Dave, 108, 110

"rat race," 19–21

relationships

competition and, 10

multidimensional winning for, 75

trust and, 149

responsibility, 151

retirement, trust and, 150

rewiring, of brain, 66–67

*Rich Dad, Poor Dad* (Kiyosaki), 25

Ries, Eric, 136

risk taking. *See* All-In

Robbins, Sage, 109

Robbins, Tony, 62–63, 109–110

Robinson, Sir Ken, 53, 181

Rohn, Jim, 139

Rosenkrantz, Jay, 145

"scaling smart," "scaling-up challenge" *versus,* 134–135, 140

seeds, of success, 170

self-development, 139–140, 225–226

self-expression

Hopkins on, 223

importance of, 41–44

moving forward through, 167

shared workspaces, 32–34, 36, 54

Share Game (FreshBiz workshop), 125

Shlain, Leonard, 212

shoelace product. *See* Hickies

Sinek, Simon, 121

Slim, Melissa, 54

Smarketing, defined, xiii

Smart Business, 113–140, *114*

building, 119

choosing location for, 35

defined, 115–117

higher mission of, 119–125

lifestyle supported by, 133–140

packaging a value for, 117–119

Smart Business (*continued*)
  price of starting a business, 40
  Win to the Winth Power with,
      126–133
Smartnership
  defined, xiii
  for Smart Business, 127–131
  Waingarten on, 208
smoking, 52
Social Gamers, 35–37
social media
  global thinking and, 36
  LinkedIn for networking, 85–86
  "pay with a tweet" concept, 86
  Smart Business and value of, 118
Social Security, trust and, 150–151
solutionaries, 53, 177–181, *178*
stock market, 5–7, 20
storytelling, 169
summer jobs, entrepreneurial, 110


*Tactics of Hope: How Social*
      *Entrepreneurs Are Changing*
      *Our World, The* (Hopkins),
      220
Tayeb, Ninet, 157, 183–188
TEDx Talks
  on "hackschooling," 151–152
  by Hewitt, 43–44
  by Sinek, 121
  "Turning Powerful Stats into Art"
      (Jordan), 52
Thiel, Peter, 103
Thiel Fellowship, 103
*Think and Grow Rich* (Hill), 119–120
Thoreau, Henry David, 34
Throw the Dice
  defined, xii
  example, 62
  moving forward and, 39
transformation, x–xii
trust
  in others, 146–152
  in yourself, 152–154

"Turning Powerful Stats into Art"
      (Jordan), 52
Twain, Mark, 38
Twitter, "pay with a tweet" concept, 86
2 Degrees Food, 126–127, 199–204


Uber, 58
United States, economy of, 51–52
"Unleash the Power Within" (Robbins),
      62–63
"unschooling," 151–152


vacation, importance of, 137–139
value
  as compensation, xi
  packaging, 117–119
  providing, 170
Vaynerchuk, Gary, 123–124
Virgin, 41, 173–175
Vroman, Jon, 19, 224–229


Waingarten, Mariquel, 28, 204–210
*Walden; or, Life in the Woods*
      (Thoreau), 34
Walters, Lauren, 126–127, 199–204
Waze, 37
Weiss, Joshua, 15, 90
wellness. *See* health
WhatsApp, 118
Wikipedia, 37
windfalls, use of, 107
*Wine Library TV* (blog), 123–124
winning, 159–175, *160*
  avoiding fear, 163–167
  creating Quantum Leaps for,
      172–175
  expectation of, 161–163
  as journey, 171–172
  potential for, 175
  self-expression for, 167
  Tayeb on success, 183–188
  tricks of New Entrepreneurz,
      167–171

Win to the Winth Power, 71–78, *72*
  as alternative to competition, 15–16
  changing mind-set for, 76
  defined, xii
  learning about Action Cards in, 84–85
  problem of competition, 73–75
  with Smart Business, 126–133
women
  feminine values, 212
  networking for, 120–121, 189–194
Woodward, Michelle, 54–55

workplace
  Action Cards for, 92
  trust and, 148–149

Zappos, 93
Zohar, Iris, 120–121, 189–194
Zoom Out
  Action Cards as leverage, 82
  Action Cards as resource, 94
  defined, xii
  optional *versus* mandatory actions, 111 (*See also* Green Titles and Red Titles)